EXPECT TO WIN

Bill Glass
EXPECT TO WIN

WORD BOOKS
PUBLISHER
WACO, TEXAS

EXPECT TO WIN

TO MY FAMILY: *Mavis, Billy, Bobby,* and *Mindy Glass.*

The truths discussed in this book were tried and proven long ago, but you were the ones upon whom my version of these eternal principles were tested. You are each winners in most every way. You always did *"Expect to Win!"* You have been and will continue to be winners because you are real BELIEVERS!

In a way, I suppose this is almost a family biography, since each step in the "ladder to your dreams" was first tried for many years with you. I dedicate this book to you because you gave these ideas the acid test. Every idea worked for you; otherwise, I wouldn't have included it in the ladder.

CONTENTS

ACKNOWLEDGMENTS

—My deep appreciation for editorial help from Fritz Ridenour and Beverly Phillips.

—Special thanks to the highly intelligent and dedicated typists of this book, Janie Walker and Ruth Hale.

—Special love and appreciation to: Garry Kinder, Jack Kinder, Zig Ziglar, Dr. William H. Cook, and Fred Smith. Your friendship and books played a large part in the shaping of my philosophy.

—Special appreciation, also, to Jarrell McCracken and WORD BOOKS for publishing all my books.

FOREWORD

by the children of Bill Glass

Ever since we were very young my father has applied the methods he discusses in this book in raising Bobby, Mindy, and me. Of course, when we were younger we would laugh about some of the things our father would harp on. But as we became older, we realized the vital importance of being positive and thinking the kind of thoughts that would propel us toward our goals.

By the time I was six my father had already impressed upon me the importance of setting goals and being specific by writing these goals down. As you might suspect, I was a little bewildered by the importance my father placed on this technique. Nonetheless, I took him very seriously and wrote down what I wanted to be as a six-year-old. And when I became seven, I did the same thing. Then I began to write down not only ultimate goals, but immediate and intermediate goals. I continue to do this today, and I plan to the rest of my life. I also found, when I was quite young, that by speaking positive words about my endeavors, they had a way of materializing. I was so sure that they were going to work that I would start talking as if my ideas or desires or plans had already come together, and amazingly enough, they would.

But even with all of these ways of thinking and these techniques for succeeding, there are always setbacks. And I was not without mine. I learned very quickly God's principle of the second mile and that there is just a lot of plain, old, hard work that accompanies success of any magnitude. The law of the second mile briefly says if one mile is required, then go two. I think this is one of the most applicable principles in the Bible because it implies two things immediately: one, as Christians, God expects us to do the best possible job in all things we attempt; two, there's a right kind of attitude we should take as Christians— one of willingness to do whatever it takes to accomplish what we attempt and to do it with as much enthusiasm as possible.

God has blessed me in a fantastic manner. I am in my first year with the Cincinnati Bengals where I play guard and center for punts and extra points. I am convinced that my station in life did not just occur. You see, when I was six, the goal that I wrote down on that piece of paper stated exactly the occupation which I'm in now. I am positive that these principles will work for you and for anyone who is willing to *Expect to Win*.

BILLY GLASS
Cincinnati, Ohio

*   *   *

I've always thought of myself as being able to do anything that I wanted to do. Dad started teaching me at a very young age how to think good thoughts. I really didn't understand the importance of doing this until I grew older and my life started falling into place perfectly, in most areas. I have to "blame" it on positive thinking. I have also learned that saying good words has helped me. You can think about yourself as becoming success-ful, but actually putting positive words in the air and saying them aloud so you can hear them helps you build confidence.

This should be a private thing. For example, if you go around saying you are great all the time, people will think you are arro-gant. Every time you are by yourself, rehearse your goals and keep telling yourself you can reach them. A person must have goals and should write them down on paper where he or she can read them daily. When I was trying to put on weight and increase my speed in junior high and high school, at my Dad's suggestion, I wrote down all my measurements and my 40-yard dash time. Then I waited a month and compared the figures. It always encouraged me when I improved. But, I never let myself be satisfied. I'm still trying to improve by being specific in setting my goals. Life would be boring without goals.

When I was a senior in high school, I developed a severe infection in my lower hip. As a result, I couldn't walk, much less play football. I was trying to have a great season so I could get a college scholarship. I was heartbroken and honestly "mad" at God. But after praying and thinking about it, I realized that God had a plan in this for me. In the meantime, I was out of commission.

God started to show me why he was putting me through this. He taught me that without him, I was nothing, and to remember that everything he had given me could easily be taken away. He taught me how to treat other people. I had no time for anybody before. All I had thought about was playing football. I finally realized that this was the price I was going to have to pay to learn these lessons about the Christian life. I was told there was no way I would ever run well enough to play football again. However, the Lord helped me to *never quit trying*. At times the pain was unbearable, maybe not as much physically as mentally. At times I thought I was going to have a mental breakdown. I can remember crying myself to sleep many times at night. People kept saying, "Glass, just forget about it. There are other things you can do."

I learned to use the hurt I felt as a motivating factor by storing it in a "little box" in the back of my mind and saying to myself, "I'll show them." After two years of going to doctors, working on weights, thinking good thoughts, and praying for something good to happen, I made it. The Lord let me "have my cake" (which I think was the lesson I learned), and "eat it too" (still getting to play football). I now am the starting offensive right tackle for the Baylor Bears. Praise the Lord!

BOBBY GLASS
Waco, Texas

* * *

My dad has always encouraged us to be positive. He would say, "If you're thinking failure, it's bad, but if you go so far as to actually say it out loud, you're programming yourself to fail." I can remember when I was younger and my dad constantly told me how great I was and how I could do anything I set my mind to. All I had to do was pick something out and I'd be a success. My brothers and I would laugh and make fun of Dad and all his positive talk. I really didn't believe it was that important. But I'm here to tell you after being in the homes of some of my friends and seeing how their parents cut them down, I see that encouraging words are extremely important!

As a result of my parents' influence, I "expect to win" and I know this attitude helps me in all aspects of life. I feel that my friends enjoy being around me, because I make a habit of building them up, while most people cut them down. I've noticed that people are a little like my dog—they wait to be patted on the head. Although people aren't as obvious about it as a dog, I can tell this is really what they need.

I'm certainly not yet the kind of Christian person I dream of being, but I've always had a thought somewhere in the back of my mind that I definitely will accomplish my goals in life. Even as I'm writing this, it sounds vain for me to think I'm always going to win, but it's that crazy little thought that drives me to many of my victories.

MINDY GLASS
Midlothian, Texas

INTRODUCTION

It is okay to be a winner.

Perhaps that sounds odd, but I say it for a good reason. Among many Christians there is what might be called an "anti-winning syndrome." The idea is that if we are trying to be a winner, we are somehow less spiritual, less dedicated to serving God. A desire for winning is often linked to pride and a lack of humility.

But it all depends on what we mean by being a winner. The Christian wants to be a winner at living an effective Christian life, not at gaining the acclaim of a worldly, secular system. God promised Joshua "good success" if he would make the Scriptures his guide for life (see Josh. 1:8, 9).

A big part of living an effective Christian life is doing our jobs efficiently. The Scriptures tell us, "Whatever your hand finds to do, do it with all your might" (Eccles. 9:10, NIV). As a Cleveland Brown, it was my job to be the very best defensive end that I could possibly be. That meant dominating the tackle against whom I was playing, overpowering him, and cutting down the ball carrier as he tried to go through me or rushing the quarterback and sacking him before he could get off a pass. But I had to do all of this with my whole heart. People just aren't interested in a half-hearted defensive end. So my influence as a Christian is much stronger as a successful defensive end.

And it takes a whole-hearted effort to be a winner in whatever profession you enter.

Not only is it okay for a Christian to be a success, but I believe it is a Christian's responsibility to be as successful as possible. Mediocrity is sinful, just as sinful as a lack of humility or a lack of depending upon God's grace and power. I have a strong belief in the grace of God and depend upon his power in my life, but this does not mean I can be lazy in carrying out my daily assignments. I must take responsibility for my own action and realize that God holds me accountable.

There is a great deal of truth in Grantland Rice's words, "The important thing is not whether you win or lose, but how you play the game." But there is a deep inbred desire in all of us to be winners. We may play the game well and that's fine. But occasionally, we must win. There is a sense in which we are winning as we are progressively moving toward our worthwhile goal. If we can't experience some type of victory, life becomes extremely drab. If we can feel deep within that we have achieved, our personality comes alive.

The concepts in this book are practical things that have been taught for centuries. Most of them are based directly on Scripture. The Bible talks about the importance of thinking right thoughts, speaking good words, being willing to take responsibility, going the second mile, expecting to win, and never giving up.

Obviously, if we rely only on these concepts and not on Christ, the concepts will deteriorate into dull, deadly humanism. But when these ideas are invigorated by the power and presence of the Holy Spirit, they are the key to powerful, effective living. We must try to make these practical success ideas blend perfectly with our sincere Christian commitment.

The simple but basic principles in this book can mold your life, if you are willing to make them part of your very being. Every one of these principles is a winning idea, if we have the discipline to use it daily, sometimes hourly.

A weight lifter does not rebel against repetition of the tried and proven methods of weight lifting. If he does, his body remains undeveloped. In the same way, you cannot disregard winning ideas and expect to be a winner. The great Vince Lombardi said, "Don't tell me about trick plays and new formations! When the crisis comes in the game, I want to know one thing: Will that team block and tackle?" You must go back to the basic fundamentals of Scripture and repeat them over and over again in your life until they become a permanent part of your thinking and behavior. Once these principles become very much a part of you, you can expect to win! You can expect to be propelled to your goals. And the mere expectation is part of the secret to their realization.

Back in 1936, Jessie Owens came back from the Olympic Games as the World's Fastest Man. At a huge press conference, the first question asked was, "How did you do it, Jessie? Four gold medals, you embarrassed Hitler in his own hometown, the fastest man in the world . . . how did you do it?"

"Oh," he said, "I think it all began when I was just a kid back in junior high school, and my coach got us all together and made a speech I've never forgotten. The main thing he said was, 'You can pretty well become whatever you make up your mind to be.'

"As a junior high kid, I looked up at my coach and shouted, 'Coach, I've already decided what I want to be! The fastest man in the world!' And my coach looked down at me, a little skinny, scrawny black boy and said, 'Jessie, that's a great dream. Fact is, Jessie, I don't know if I've ever heard such a great dream as that. There's only one problem with your dream, Jessie.'

" 'What's that, coach?'

" 'Dreams have a way of floating high in the sky. They just float up there like clouds. Dreams never become realities unless you have the courage to build a ladder to them.'

" 'How do you build a ladder to a dream, coach?'

" 'Well, Jessie,' he said, 'you build it one step at a time.' "

Even those incredible trips to the moon and back took a first step!

In this book I discuss nine steps which I have found to be a basic part of my dream ladder. I'm sure you are aware of all of them, but I guarantee that if you'll follow them step by step, they'll definitely make your dreams come true! However, if you fail to follow them, or even skip one rung on the ladder, your dreams will turn to clouds and rain on your parade. But determined step-by-step climbing can make your fantasy a reality. Indeed, you can "expect to win" in the very best sense!

1.

THINK RIGHT
THOUGHTS

The First Rung of the Ladder Is to Think Right

Thinkers down through the centuries have disagreed on almost everything. There is only one point upon which they have all agreed: "People become what they think about."

We need to be careful what we think, because what we think becomes reality in our lives. The first time I ever ran across that idea was back in high school. My high school English teacher told us that Emerson had said, "Man becomes what he thinks about all day long." I applied some of my teenage logic to this and said to myself, "Emerson was quite a guy. Man becomes what he thinks about all day long—what a fantastic thought! But if that's true—if I become what I think about all day long, I'll be a girl!" Obviously, I'm exaggerating, but you can see my point.

Of course, thinking about girls isn't what Emerson had in mind. He was really outlining the key to living. Living starts with a mental picture of what you would like to be someday. Florence Nightingale dreamed of being a nurse. Edison pictured himself as an inventor. People who accomplish great things have escaped the mere shove of circumstance by imagining a future so vividly that they have been able to reach seemingly impossible goals.

Albert Einstein said, "Imagination is everything. It is the preview of life's coming attractions." And this works both positively and negatively.

Think Garbage and You Get Garbage

One of the most potent proverbs in the Scriptures tells us that as a man "thinketh in his heart, so is he" (Prov. 23:7). The context of that verse talks about a stingy host who is begrudging his guests the food he is serving, but the application of the verse is practically universal. As we think in our hearts, so we become. That is why pornography can be so damaging. We Americans spend eight billion dollars each year on pornography, and then we wonder why we have so many dirty results! We really shouldn't be surprised. If we put garbage in our minds, we become garbage cans. We have no reason to be surprised. If someone were to go into your living room and pour out a large can of slimy garbage, you might suggest they clean it up. If you were big enough, you might "insist" they clean it up. And yet so many of us encourage other people to pour cans of slimy garbage into our minds all the time. Rather than saying, "Don't put that garbage in my mind," we say, "Give me more, give me more." I'm not only talking about the garbage of dirty pictures on paper; I'm also talking about the garbage of unbelief. Faith is belief in something before it happens. A lack of it can be deadly.

Think how devastating this is to the pass receiver who sees himself missing the ball when he hears his number called in the huddle. If he had faith, he could see himself catch the ball! Think of the man who sees himself fail in a sales opportunity. He will no doubt fail.

Lack of faith is even more destructive in relation to God. Belief in God is the only thing that can keep us from ultimate despair. Only the sense of the grace of God can keep us from giving up on ourselves; and only the sense of the overruling providence of God can keep us from despairing about our world.

The hope of the Christian is indestructible because it is founded on the eternal God.

In the Sermon on the Mount, Christ taught that sins are not only acts, but thoughts. "You have heard that it was said to the people long ago, 'Do not murder . . .' But I tell you that anyone who is angry with his brother will be subject to judgment. . . . You have heard that it was said, 'Do not commit adultery.' But I tell you that anyone who looks at a woman lustfully has already committed adultery with her in his heart" (Matt. 5:21–22, 27–28, NIV).

Here, Christ is speaking of the Old Testament law which governs overt actions but has little to say about the heart. He says we are now responsible for our thoughts as well as our acts. I suppose one of the reasons Christ gave us these deeper looks into the law is that he understands our humanity so well. Our make-up is such that the mind works its will upon us. Vivid pictures in the mind become realities ultimately, if not immediately. Temptation starts with something we picture in our minds. Samson could only see the beauty of Delilah. It's too bad his mental pictures didn't include her betrayal with a kiss! Fortunately, we have a powerful weapon to defeat temptation. We can stop temptation in the thought stage and keep it from moving into the more destructive "acting" stage.

Christ is telling us that the minute an evil or tempting thought crosses our minds, we should face it, admit it, confess it, and forsake it. Then it can never become an ugly reality. Christ here gives us not only a principle to have victory over temptation, but a secret to successful living. Using this key, we can defeat sin and program ourselves to success!

Imagination Has Unlimited Power

Henry J. Kaiser maintained that "you can imagine your future," and he believed that a great part of his business success was due to daydreams. Harry S. Truman said that he used daydreaming for rest and recuperation. "I have a foxhole in my mind," he used to say. Conrad Hilton dreamed of operating a hotel in his boyhood. He recalled that all his accomplishments were first realized in his imagination.

The Apollo astronauts, when preparing to go to the moon, practiced daily in imagination, from liftoff to splashdown. When Neil Armstrong first set foot on the moon, he said that he was astounded at how much the whole experience was like he had imagined it would be. "Just like our drills!" he exclaimed. "It was exactly as we imagined it would be." They had practiced every day. They had played "Let's Go to the Moon" thousands of times. The rest is history.

Hold a picture of yourself long and strong enough in your mind's eye, and you will be drawn toward it. Picture yourself vividly as defeated and that alone will make you a loser. Picture yourself as a winner and that will contribute immeasurably to success. Don't picture yourself as anything, and you will drift aimlessly.

Why do vivid mental pictures help us to achieve the success we want? There is a basic psychological reason for this. Dr. Maxwell Maltz, a well-known plastic surgeon and author of *Psycho-Cybernetics*, says that our nervous systems can't tell the difference between an imagined experience and a real experience.[1] So it is, then, that our computer-like subconsciouses accept as fact whatever is fed to them whether the images are negative or positive.

Thought Power at the "Hanoi Hilton"

During the Vietnamese conflict, hundreds of American flyers were held captive in the "Hanoi Hilton," as they called it. Some of them were there as long as nine years. Most of them were there three to five years. During the long monotony of those months and years of deprivation and torture, loneliness and suffer-

---

1. Maxwell Maltz, *Psycho-Cybernetics*, (Englewood Cliffs, N.J.: Prentice Hall, Inc., 1960).

ing, they maintained a sense of balance and sanity. How did they do it? They turned the concentration camp into a university for personal development. They weren't simply trying to cope or just exist. They were using their time. They became better people, rather than worse, for having gone through the prison experience.

Many of them learned foreign languages from each other. Others got together and quoted verses of Scripture which they knew, then memorized the composite of all the verses which everyone could recall. Not having a real Bible, they had to make one up in their memories.

Perhaps most amazing of all, they learned to play musical instruments while "guests" of the North Vietnamese government. Not having any real instruments, they imagined the keyboard or the banjo strings, and became very proficient instrumentalists, though no sounds came from the imagined instruments.

Colonel George Hall returned from Vietnam a proficient golfer, though he had been golfing only in his imagination. Only a duffer prior to being in the concentration camp, he imagined himself playing. He played with a daydreamed set of clubs on a fantasized course. But he imagined it all in vivid color. He would step up on the tee box, place the ball on the tee, get into proper position, take just the right stance, and use a beautiful backstroke and follow-through. His chip-shots, his putting, and his whole game were practiced in his mind literally millions of times. When Colonel Hall returned to the United States, he entered the New Orleans Open only one week after his release and shot a seventy-six. An astounding score for a man who hadn't touched a real club for seven years! The world of the imagination is boundless and without limitation. What we put into our minds tends to come back in our life exactly as we have planted it there. Other men built houses and ran businesses utilizing mental pictures like Hall did, and then did them in reality when they returned home.

Airline pilots cannot afford mistakes. Therefore, they have

to be thoroughly experienced before ever flying an airplane. This can only be done in a simulator. The simulator takes the best of imagination and parts of reality without the risk of failure, and produces proficiency that assures safety in flying.

The Key to Success or Failure

It's not what we think we *are* that holds us back, but what we think we are *not*. What we think is really what we are. If we engage in self-talk like, "I have a lousy memory;" "I'm poor in math;" "I'm a poor cook;" "I'm never on time;" or "I'm a true Leo," these become self-fulfilling prophecies. I've noticed hundreds of prison inmates who have tattoos on their bodies that read, "Born to Lose." We never outgrow the limits we place on ourselves. Our computer-like subconsciouses don't judge "good/bad, true/untrue, right/wrong." They are simply obedient servants guiding us swiftly toward our goals.

Since 90 percent of the brain is subconscious, it is therefore important that it be properly programmed. There is awesome power in the subconscious mind. Take, for example, the mother who comes out of her house and sees her son pinned beneath a car after a jack has fallen. This 114-pound mother runs to the car and picks it up while her son crawls out. You say, "This is impossible." But no one ever told her it was, and her subconscious mind obediently helped her to perform the impossible.

We can't really erase negative programming. Knowing that failure pictures tend to reproduce themselves, you may say, "Oh, I can't think that way. I must not think of myself failing." But this doesn't help; it only drives the failure picture that much deeper into your mind, making it more likely to recur. It just makes you more likely to do what you don't want to do. It's like the coach telling the player not to fumble. It makes him just that much more likely to fumble!

Since it can't be erased, it must be replaced with a success picture. If we picture what we want to happen often enough, it will actualize itself.

So, if a negative picture comes into our minds, we must replace it with a positive picture. What I'm really suggesting is that we must put worry in reverse. Worry is picturing what we don't want to happen, and I am suggesting that we simply picture what we want to happen instead.

Paul Realized the Power of the Mind

The Apostle Paul obviously knew nothing of modern self-image psychology. Psycho-cybernetics came two thousand years after Paul. Today there is a whole field of literature which teaches that the mind is something like a heat-seeking missile. It tends to lock in on those pictures we hold firmly in our imagination. Yet, this great apostle was well aware of the tremendous power of the mind when it is fixed on a certain target. He writes, "Finally, brethren, whatsoever things are true, whatsoever things are honest, whatsoever things are just, whatsoever things are pure, whatsoever things are lovely, whatsoever things are of good report, if there be any virtue, and if there be any praise, think on these things" (Phil. 4:8).

This verse is a powerful suggestion for the right way to live. We should think about things that are true, right, and excellent, and how to achieve them. This wisdom is the key to a spiritual psycho-cybernetics. It is a way to lock our minds on target, and it will assure the realization of our goals.

The human mind will always set itself on something. Paul is trying to tell us that we should be careful to keep our minds on the right things. Thoughts will be literally grooved, and it is difficult to ever jerk them out of the subconscious mind. Some authorities seem to say that it is impossible. At the very least, we have to reprogram the mind so that it is working for us. That is why Paul is so emphatic in saying that it is important for a person to set his thoughts on positive things! He even makes a list of what those things should be. Of course, this list isn't personalized, but it is specific enough that, with some small amount of work, we can make a very personal list of ways to think concerning our own goals.

There are things that are obviously wrong for us to think about, and this passage in Philippians encourages us to pull our minds out of those channels, and put them on things that are right and good and noble.

The word translated "lovely" in this verse can also be translated "attractive" or "winsome." Paraphrased, it would be "that which calls forth love." Life is like an echo—you get back what you put out. There are those whose minds are set on vengeance. I have met many of them in prison. Because of this, they produce in others bitterness and fear. There are those whose minds are set on criticism and rebuke, and they call forth in others resentment and a lack of trust. The mind of the Christian should be set on lovely things—kindness, sympathy, forbearance—so that he will be a "winsome" person, one who calls forth love in others. When we think in these ways, we are able to pass this special gift of God on to others. But before we can pass it along to others, we must first make sure that we apply it to our own lives, letting it change us so completely that we, like Paul, can suggest that others can follow in our footsteps. Few teachers or preachers can speak like this, yet it remains true that personal example is an essential part of teaching. The teacher must demonstrate in action the truth which he expresses in words. He is not only passing on a body of doctrine, but also living it out in personal interpretation.

You may say, "But be practical! How do I focus on what is 'honorable?' " Try thinking of ways in which you can care about others, ways you can go out of your way to be helpful, ways to keep your word, ways to show respect for the feelings of other people, and ways to help someone without letting anyone know about it.

If you want to think the right thoughts in the right ways, make Philippians 4:8 your life verse—the verse that means the most to you, the one you constantly quote to yourself.

Athletes Make Maximum Use of Imagination

I lockered next to Jim Brown, the greatest fullback that ever lived, for seven years. One day in a game against New York, he gained 232 yards. After the game, I said, "Jim, how did you gain 232 yards in one game? That's fantastic! How did you get yourself so 'up'?" He hesitantly revealed, "All week long before we played against New York, I saw myself in my imagination doing my job. I saw myself ripping up the middle, catching passes, making blocks, and doing everything I was going to do in the game, and when the game finally came and I did those things well, I wasn't surprised." Isn't that it? Isn't a large part of athletic success in the imagination of the athlete himself? He sees himself in his mind's eye doing his job well before the game. When he is in the game, he does well and he isn't surprised. The mental tapes simply play themselves back.

Gary Player, the great golfer, is one of the most dedicated visualizers in the athletic world. He imagines every shot prior to making the shot. And if he should make a bad shot, he stops and imagines himself making the shot ten times in the proper way. He replaces all his negative pictures with positive ones.

During his baseball career, Ted Williams, one of the all-time greats of the game, had outstanding season batting averages of .400 and .389. Evidently he was doing something right! In explaining the secret of his success, he says, "I always sat in the dugout, or in the batting circle, or on the plane or train thinking of the game. And it was always the same. I imagined myself hitting the ball over and over again. Prior to the game, I imagined, in vivid detail, just what I would do in the game. It happened just as I'd imagined it would."

We can actually daydream our successes long before we realize them. In sports, John Uelses, former pole-vaulting champ, made deliberate use of daydreaming. Before each meet he visualized winning and vividly saw himself clearing the bar at a certain height. He repeatedly went over not only all the minute details of the act of winning, but saw the stadium, the crowds, and even smelled the grass and the earth. He maintained that the resulting memory traces influenced his actual performance during the meet.

Drs. Penfield and Roberts at the Montreal Institute of Neurology discovered that they could touch a certain point in the brain with electrodes and the patient would relive experiences from the past. I didn't say they would "remember"; they actually "relived" the experience with all the same sights, sounds, and even smells.

Since everything that has happened or that has been vividly imagined is stored in the brain, it is important that we carefully guard what we allow in, because what goes in will most certainly come out.

It is so easy to prostitute the mind by negative programming. I once knew a man who had a great mind, but was constantly preoccupied with trivia. His whole life was lived in excitement over nothing. This reminds me of the line from *Macbeth* which describes life as "filled with sound and fury, signifying nothing."

It's Not Only What You Think, But How You Think It

I became so convinced of the power of the mind that I engaged in a project that had monumental impact on my performance in football. I made tapes of little talks to myself, about seven minutes in length, on my recorder. The cassette sounded like this:

"Charge. Charge. Every time the word *charge* floats through your mind, it will activate all the suggestions on this tape. Dominate your opponent. Dominate him. Fire across the line, overpower him. Feel his body crumble beneath your power. Throw him down on the inside, rush to the outside, and sack the quarterback. Pursue, pursue, pursue. Pursue until you hear the whistle. On running downs, destroy the blocker. Fire through the ball carrier. . . ."

On and on the tape went for seven minutes, filled with powerful, positive suggestions concerning things I would accomplish during the game. I was convinced that this type of programming would promote mental pictures that would gravitate toward my playing in a super way. These suggestions would program my subconscious mind and during the game they would be "played back" when I said the word *charge* to myself. "Charge!" would be the mental electrode that would trigger the powerful suggestions in the tape. So, I listened to that tape in the mornings several times on my way to work, before going to bed, and over and over again all week long prior to the game.

But something went wrong. In the game, I played the most horrible football I've ever played in my life! In the film-study session the following Tuesday morning, the coaches were yelling and screaming at me, saying, "You hit an all-time low! You were terrible!"

After viewing the film of that particular game, I went out of the film-study session smiling. You might ask, "Why were you smiling after playing such a horrible game and getting chewed out by your coaches?" It had dawned on me in the study of the films that *I was playing precisely in the way I had put the suggestions into my subconscious.* I had said, "Charge. Charge," in a rather hypnotic tone, and the whole mood of the tape was in a monotone—almost as if I was just waltzing through the assignments when game time came. Sure enough, I was waltzing through my assignments and gliding through my responsibilities in a sleepy manner. I knew if I could change the tone of the tapes, I would also be able to change the way I would perform in the game.

I went back to my room, and began to develop a new recording. This time the tape was literally shouting with emotion and power. "CHARGE! CHARGE! Every time the word *charge* explodes out of your mouth, it will activate all the suggestions on this tape! DOMINATE YOUR OPPONENT! DOMINATE HIM! . . ." It was done in explosive bursts of energy with great enthusiasm and shouting.

The next week, we played against St. Louis. All week long, I listened to the tapes of shouted commands many times every day, and finally I was on my way to the game with the team. I made a deal with myself that I would listen to the tape repeatedly until we arrived in St. Louis. We flew for about an hour and a half aboard a chartered plane, and when we reached St. Louis, it was fogged in. So, we circled St. Louis for another hour and a half, and wound up flying to Chicago, where we boarded a bus and slowly journeyed all the way back to St. Louis. It took us a total of 13 hours to get there, and I listened to this tape the entire time. I rewound and played it literally hundreds of times until I feared it would collapse with fatigue, or the batteries would wear out. But I discovered a great truth. Consciously, we tire of hearing the same thing over and over again, but the subconscious never tires. Repetition simply reinforces the message.

The next day, I was literally brainwashed with the commands recorded on my tape. I overpowered my opponent and dominated him as the tape suggested. I pursued him until the whistle. I started doing things I'd never done before. I rushed the passer early in the game. Just as I was about to sack him, he released a short pass. The receiver caught the ball and ran zig-zagging for the goal line. I pursued even though I normally would have been satisfied with the pressure I applied to the quarterback, without chasing the receiver. He was delayed by eluding tacklers and I tackled him seventy yards downfield. In the film-study session, the coaches raved about my making a tackle seventy yards downfield after rushing the quarterback. It was programmed in so well that it was a reflex action. I was operating like an efficient robot performing obediently according to my programming.

Maybe that was the norm. I was simply discovering the mechanism of God's creation. He has equipped me with a guidance system called the "subconscious." This system is instructed through the picture-producing brain. These images are stored and played back on cue. What we call "luck," good or bad, is just the tape we happen to trigger in the subconscious which plays back just as it went in. The trick is to put only positive tapes into your mind. That is the only way to insure your results.

Finally, three plays before this game was over, I literally fainted in exhaustion. But I can honestly say that I've never played such fantastic football in my life. You see, my subconscious mind had pushed me to carry out the suggestions on the tape, precisely as I had imagined.

In a sport like football, it's important to play subconsciously. Getting in tune with the inner self and playing back the right tapes at the right time become second nature. But we also need God's presence to empower us professionally and otherwise. The two aren't working in conflict, but in a partnership of spiritual and psychological strength.

Paul would have agreed with what I learned with my football tapes. It isn't just *what* you think, but *how* you think it. This is especially true of the spiritual life. We might have all the right answers, biblically and doctrinally, but unless we have real enthusiasm and real dedication and devotion to Christ, we will play a rather robotlike game, and we will "waltz" through our Christian assignments, and not be as successful as we could be.

When you are filled with the Holy Spirit, many of these reactions come out of your innermost parts like "rivers of living water."

How to Make This Step on the Ladder Work

1. Remember, people become what they think about.
2. Put aside ten or fifteen minutes every day for daydreaming, or what some people would call "biblical meditation." Run Philippians 4:8 through your mind. Visualize your future and relive past success experiences. If failure pictures come into your mind, replace them with success pictures. The two key words are *relive* and *replace.*
3. Pray at least an equal amount of time about the subject of your daydreams. Then go out and make it happen by God's grace and power. Don't *let* it happen—*make* it happen!
4. Make a list of good things, worthy things upon which to

think concerning the ten most important goals in your life. Study
Philippians 4:8 for guidelines in coming up with these specifics.
Then transfer these to your prayer list.

5. Remember, thoughts are like seeds planted in the brain.
Not only do they grow and bear fruit, but they *must* multiply!

2.

SAY GOOD WORDS

The Second Rung of the Ladder Is What You Say

Mohammed Ali used to say, "I am the greatest, I am the greatest, I am the greatest." He said it so many times that he started to believe it himself. Even his opponents tended to agree. He would predict the round in which he planned to knock out his opponent, and the opponent would cooperate! What you say has a peculiar way of becoming fact.

I can hear what you're thinking. You're saying, "What you say isn't so important as what you do. No one is impressed with a lot of talk with little action." Obviously, a person who talks ahead of his actions is laughed at. Some people do use talk rather than actions. "Since I can't play a good game, I talk a good game." However, in the sincere person, words tend to actualize themselves. What you say has a fantastic influence on what you become, and how you affect others.

What We Say Conditions Our Minds

Solomon—the wisest of men—knew the power in words. In Proverbs 18:20 (NIV), he said, "From the fruit of his mouth a man's stomach is filled; with the harvest from his lips he is satisfied."

Solomon is saying that positive speech satisfies a person. Say good things. Tell yourself you can do it—and it will happen. We have already seen an example of this in Mohammed Ali. But he isn't the only one who has been "satisfied by the harvest of his lips."

After talking to the Texas Rangers baseball team about this subject, their star catcher, Jim Sundberg, came up to me and said, "You know, Bill, what you say is true. When I was just a kid, my dad always told me I'd end up as a great major league catcher." Then smiling in an almost little boyish way, he added, "I didn't let my daddy down!"

The 1980 Miss America was Cheryl Prewitt. I heard her say that when she was only four or five years old, she hung around her father's small, country grocery store. Almost daily the milkman would come, and she would follow him to watch as he lined the display cases with shiny bottles of milk. He always greeted her with, "How's my little Miss America?" At first she giggled, but she soon became comfortable with it. Before long, it was a childhood fantasy, then a teenage dream, and finally, a solid goal. It all started with a word spoken daily to a young, impressionable mind. It became imbedded in the subconscious. It became a prayer and a reality. Who was responsible: the milkman, the subconscious of a growing child, or God? I'd say all three, but lean toward God, because he created them all.

Solomon gives us more food for thought in Proverbs 18:21 where he says: "The tongue has the power of life and death, and those who love it will eat its fruit" (NIV).

The tongue has the power of life. It can bring us success in building part of that ladder to our dreams. Or, it has the power to bring death.

I recently went to a wedding of a friend of my son's. My son and his friends had all been on the high school football team. Bobby was best man, and there were seven groomsmen, all of which had been on that same team. Athletes have a code of being "good ol' boys" and just themselves. As they stepped out of the rented limousines in which they arrived, dressed in rented tuxedos that were rather ill-fitting and uncomfortably worn, I knew they must have felt foolish. They had huge ruffles on their lapels, pink shirts that were ruffly and stuck out beyond their red tuxedos. Most of them were rather large young men and walked with an embarrassed stride. I had arrived early and was standing in the foyer of the church. As they were approaching me, thoughts were flooding my mind as to what I should say. Maybe I should say, "You girls really look great in those monkey suits!" or "You guys look like a bunch of hogs in silk stockings!" or something else to poke fun at them. But then I remembered the importance of words, so I thought to myself, "How do they feel, with their athletic backgrounds and small-town reverence for being yourself, and unsophisticated orientation? They are embarrassed, uncomfortable, unsure of themselves, immature, and what they most need right now is a positive word of reinforcement and encouragement." And so I said, "You guys have never looked greater! You should wear tuxedos more often!"

For the remainder of the evening, every time I turned around, those young men were looking for an excuse to talk to me— being friendly, asking questions about me and my family, and sharing some of their goals and dreams for the future. Positive words have a fantastic impact on our total being. People everywhere are dying to hear positive words of reinforcement! And these young men were no different.

I do a lot of work in prisons. In the last eight years, I have been in 150 institutions. I have done so much time in prisons I could rob one bank "free"!

Over the years, I've talked to thousands of men behind bars. I ask them, "How many of you had a father, mother or guardian who told you you'd end up in prison?" Ninety percent of the inmates say, "My dad always told me I'd end up behind bars, and I didn't let him down."

When I repeated this idea at a women's penitentiary in South Carolina, a female inmate came up to my wife and said, "You know, what your husband says is the truth. When I was just a little kid, people would do things I didn't like, and I'd say to them, 'I'm gonna kill you.' I continued to say this, and I got to where I'd repeat it with a little more vehemence each time. I finally realized I'd never be satisfied until I murdered someone. When I finally did kill someone, it felt good." She had brainwashed herself into murder.

The worst "putdown" in the world is not the one that someone else lays on us. The most devastating words are the ones that we lay on ourselves! We can survive if someone else puts us down, but if we put ourselves down, that's difficult to overcome.

I've heard a lot of people say, "I just have a bad memory"; "I am bad at math"; "I can't cook very well"; "I'm a born loser." And they are sabotaging their own efforts by what they say.

To say, "I can't" or "I'm not" continually is a powerful drug of defeat that slows you down and limits your progress. I don't think you ought to go around imitating Mohammed Ali saying, "I am the greatest, I am the greatest . . ." all the time, but on the other hand, you ought to talk in a way that honors the fantastic job God did when he made you. Every time you say you can't, what you are really saying is, "God, you did a sorry job when you made me. I'm a mess." Nothing could be further from the truth! God did a marvelous job when he made you. The problem has come since you took over, because of your lack of belief in what God did in creating you in the first place.

Replace the "I can'ts" and "I'm nots" with the words of Solomon's father, David, who says, "For you created my inmost being; you knit me together in my mother's womb. I praise you because I am fearfully and wonderfully made; your works are wonderful, I know that full well" (Ps. 139:13–14, NIV).

What We Say Conditions Those Around Us

Not only do our words affect what we do, and how well we succeed, but what we say has a powerful effect on others.

The Green Bay Packers won three world's championships after they were "a bunch of old men." Sportswriters said there was no way Green Bay could win again, but they did in 1965, 1966 and 1967.

Later they were asked, "How did you guys do it? We thought you were all too old."

They said, "We don't know, but we think it has something to do with this guy we have on our team by the name of Willie Davis. Every time you ask Willie how he feels, he says, 'I feel good. I got that winning feeling. I feel great.' "

Willie Davis felt good so much that they conferred upon him a doctor's degree in "feeling good," and he became known as "Dr. Feelgood" all over the National Football League. Willie knew exactly what Solomon meant in Proverbs 18:21: "The tongue has the power of life . . . and those who love it will eat its fruit" (NIV).

One person's tongue can influence another in the strangest ways. I was reading not too long ago about Warren Spahn who pitched in the 1958 World Series for the Milwaukee Braves against the New York Yankees. With the series tied 3–3 at the last game, the score in this last game was also tied 3–3. Warren was pitching for Milwaukee against New York. The Yankees had a great hitter named Elston Howard.

It was the last half of the last inning of the last game, and Warren Spahn was getting ready to throw the ball, when the manager jumped out of the dugout and called time out. He walked out on the mound, kicked the dirt a couple of times, and said, "Don't throw the high-outside one." He turned and walked back to the dugout. Spahn said to himself, "Why did he tell me that? He knows I won't throw a high-outside one. Everybody knows that's the pitch Elston Howard hits over the fence. No one would be so stupid as to do that. Why would he break my concentration and tell me not to throw a high-outside one?!"

Spahn wound up and threw the ball, and do you know where it went? Right. High and outside. Elston Howard hit it so hard it was still going up as it cleared the centerfield fence.

Warren Spahn says to this day the reason he threw that high-outside pitch was because the manager planted in his mind *what he didn't want him to do*. Said Spahn, "I didn't want to throw that pitch, but I was programmed to do it—I couldn't help it." The currently dominant thought is the one that guides you.

Negative programming doesn't happen only to athletes. Parents are guilty of it all the time.

I was in a restaurant in New Mexico, and the waitress was saying to me, "Oh, that is such a fine young family over there." She was speaking of a doctor and his family, who had recently moved to town. He was a good-looking man, with a beautiful wife and little boy—truly a delightful family. But as they were eating, I heard the father say to his son, "You dummy!" As I ate, I couldn't help but listen to the conversation. During the course of the meal, he told his son he was an ignoramus, that he was stupid, and foolish. I thought to myself, "You may be a learned doctor, but you're going to ruin your child."

Parents should be careful what they say to their children. They may think their children rarely do what they tell them, but ironically enough, when they plant negative thoughts in the minds of their children, they often wind up thinking or doing just that.

On another occasion, a mother introduced me to her children. She said, "This is my little girl. She's very timid." And the little girl stood with her finger in her mouth.

"This is my little boy. He's a bully." Sure enough, there he stood with chest out, muscles flexed, frowning like a bulldog.

"This is my other little boy. He's very dumb." There he stood with a dumb look on his face. Those children had become precisely what their mother had been prophesying.

What We Say Affects Us Spiritually

In the book of Hebrews, we read over and over again that the Holy Spirit is the High Priest of our good confession. In other words, the Holy Spirit works within us to make our faith statements a reality. Whether we utter something silently to ourselves or out loud to others, it becomes a prayer to God or a confession to our fellow-man and has a tendency to actualize itself. We must be careful what we say. God may answer it as a prayer.

Numbers 14 tells the story of the children of Israel in the wilderness and how they began to feel sorry for themselves. In their murmuring, they said, "We're out here in the wilderness, and we're all going to die. This is terrible. We're all going to die." Over and over again they said that they were going to die in the wilderness. God responded with, ". . . as ye have spoken in mine ears, so will I do to you: Your carcases shall fall in this wilderness . . ." (vv. 28–29).

What if they'd said, "We're going to live and prosper out here in this wilderness"? I think they would have lived. But what happened? They died because they said they were going to. What we say becomes a confession to fellow-man and a prayer to God.

In the Book of Revelation, we see that the devil is the low priest of our negative confession. When we visualize what we don't want to happen in our minds, Satan has a way of making it come true. Worry is visualizing what we don't want to happen.

We live in a universe that was created by the spoken word of God. In the first chapter of Genesis, verses 1, 3, 6, 9, 11, 14, 20, 24 and 26, the phrase "God said" is repeated nine times. The result is the universe. Hebrews 11:3 says, "Through faith we understand that the worlds were framed by the word of God." In Psalm 33:6 we read, "By the word of the Lord were the heavens made." So, by Scripture we know that the world was created by the spoken word of God. God spoke, and the result was the universe, with billions of galaxies and billions of stars in each one of those galaxies, all floating through space at astronomical speeds and in perfect precision.

In a world that was shaped and formed by a word, it seems obvious that the word of the height of creation, which is man, will influence the created fabric of the universe. I believe that even the word of man influences the fabric of creation. When we speak a word of unbelief, we are getting in step with the destructive Satanic forces of the universe.

Still more importantly, what we say accomplishes our salvation. The Bible says if we believe in our hearts and confess with our mouths that Jesus was raised from the dead, we shall be saved. It's what we say to the Lord that determines our salvation. As I've said before, what we say becomes a prayer to God and a confession to our fellow-man. Ultimately, this affects our salvation, our inner being, and our faith before God. It affects everything in our lives.

What We Say Reveals Our Hearts

What we say also reveals what we're thinking. In Matthew 12:34 Jesus tells us, ". . . out of the abundance of the heart the mouth speaketh." If you want to know what a person is thinking in his heart, listen for the predominance of his conversation. If he talks mostly about wicked, evil things, you can be certain this is a reflection of his heart.

Likewise, if someone talks about positive, happy things, this is also a reflection of his heart. What we think about has a way of coming to the surface. And there is nothing so revealing as a word. It doesn't take long to discover whether someone has a mind that is wholesome or one that is dirty. After only a short time of listening, we can determine whether someone's mind is kind or cruel because they are continually revealing what they are by what they say. In Matthew 12:36, Jesus says that "every idle word that men shall speak, they shall give an account thereof in the day of judgment." Idle words are the "unguarded" words. They are the words we speak without thinking. They are the words uttered when conditional restraints are removed— the words that show what we're really like on the inside.

Carefully spoken words may be calculated hypocrisy. When we are consciously on guard, we will be careful what we say, and how we say it. But when we're off guard, we will speak words that will reveal our true characters. It is quite possible for us to be publicly fine and noble, while our private utterances show another side. It is when our guard is down that we reveal our hearts. Often when we're mad, our anger reveals what we really think. If we were in cool control, we probably wouldn't say the truth. Sometimes we are the model of charm and courtesy in public because we know we are being watched. At times like this, we are deliberately careful. But when we're in our homes, we're dreadful, irritable, sarcastic, critical and unpleasant. What we say when the guard is down reveals our hearts much more than what we say at other times.

Often these unguarded words do great damage. What you say in that relaxed moment will lodge in the heart of a wounded friend and never be forgotten. Once a hurting word is spoken, nothing will bring it back. It pursues a course of damage wherever it goes.

We need to examine our words. If we will do so honestly, we will discover the state of our hearts. Remember, God does not judge us by the words we speak with care and deliberation, but by the words we speak idly when the restraints are off and the real feelings of the heart come bubbling to the surface.

Change What You Say and Change Your Life

Many people believe that what they do is more important than what they say. Nonetheless, as we have seen in this chapter, what we say has a tremendous influence on us and on others. From Proverbs 18:20 we learn that what we say conditions our minds. If we say positive things, it will help us live positive, successful lives. What we say also conditions those around us. We can program people negatively or positively by what we say to them. Parents, for example, have tremendous power to program their children with positive or negative words. Just as words influenced Jim Sundberg's life, the fate of the Green Bay Packers, the life of Miss America, the plight of the children of Israel, and inmates in prison, words are changing each of us for good or bad all the time.

In Matthew 12:34, we learn that what we say also reveals our hearts. But you can change what you say, and you can change your life. As James tells us, the tongue is like a rudder of a ship. It is small but it has tremendous power (3:4–6).

Remember, what you say is an important rung on the ladder to successful living. When you control your tongue, you can expect to win—you can change your life.

How to Make This Step on the Ladder Work

1. Think back on your conversations this past week. How did your words condition your own thinking?

2. How did your words condition others?

3. How did your words help or hinder your relationship with God?

4. Think back to words that came from your parents. Were they positive or negative?

5. What kind of self-image do you have today? Can you trace this back to your parents in any way?

6. What words have you spoken to your children?

3.

BE SPECIFIC

The Third Rung of the Ladder Is to Be Specific

If you look into the mirror each morning, having no meaningful goals for the day, you'll get what you are aiming for—NOTH-ING! You are expecting nothing meaningful from the day, you envision no great accomplishments, and you will get exactly what you expect.

It is so easy to generalize, and say, "I want to achieve my dream." But that's not specific enough.

Our subconscious is like an obedient servant. Computerlike, it guides us faithfully and unquestioningly toward our objectives. The problem is that 95 percent of us have no clear-cut goals. Only 5 percent rise above the herd because they have the audacity to write on a piece of paper exactly what they want to achieve in every area of life.

The Power of a Precise Goal

If you climb to the bridge of a ship and ask the ship's captain, "What is your next port-of-call?" he would name it. For 99 percent of the voyage, he wouldn't be able to see the port, but he would be absolutely certain that if he did the right thing day by day, he would ultimately get there. There are thousands of miles of rocky coastlines and only a few hundred feet of narrow harbor entrances. The chances that the ship will ever accidentally coast into the port-of-call are one in a billion. The chances of ever accidentally getting anywhere in life are even less.

Be specific. It is important to be clear as to what you want to accomplish in every area of life, whether it is in your physical, mental, or spiritual development. I have been challenging my own two sons to do this ever since they first expressed the desire to be pro-football players. I remember when they were little, they wanted to be six-foot-six and weigh 260 pounds because that was my size. They wanted to bench-press over 300 pounds, run a five-flat 40-yard dash, and play on an All-Star team in the Pro Bowl. Today, our oldest son, Billy, weighs 270 pounds and is six-foot-five, runs a 4.9 40-yard dash, and is already an up-and-coming pro with the Cincinnati Bengals. He has achieved almost all of his goals. He wrote them down on a piece of paper. He's surpassed every goal he wrote down to this stage, except that he is about an inch shorter than six-foot-six. This is the only thing he couldn't change. Bobby, our other son, has reached 250 pounds and is also six-foot-five. He has had the disadvantage of a hurt, which you will read about in chapters 5 and 6. This slowed him down temporarily, but has ultimately helped him achieve his goals. He is currently an outstanding player with Baylor University though the doctors thought he would never play again.

Mindy, our daughter, growing up with all this "goal-setting" going on around her, has followed the same pattern. She wanted to be a cheerleader. As a tiny little girl, she was constantly getting us to watch her as she went through her tumbling and yell maneuvers. She is now a high school cheerleader.

An amazing thing happens when you have the courage to write down a goal—it tends to become a reality. But remember, you must be specific about it. If you fail to plan, you plan to fail.

Specific Physical Goals

I run about three miles every other day. You say, "You really like to run?" No, I hate every step of it, but I know I have to do it if I'm going to be in shape. My wife runs about a mile and a half every day. She's lost about four inches in her hips in the last few years.

You might say, "Physical fitness can be carried too far." And that's right. I heard about a guy who would run up and jerk a cigarette out of a man's mouth, stomp it out on the ground, and say, "Don't you know that those filthy things will give you cancer?" For twenty years, every time he'd see someone smoking, he'd run over, grab the cigarette, and stomp it out, telling them, "These filthy things cause cancer!" After twenty years of doing this, he finally died of cancer of the foot. It *can* be carried too far, but most of the time, it's not carried far enough. Everyone should be in shape physically. It's a sin against God if we fail to plan for the continuing development of our bodies.

Specific Mental Goals

It is also important to set goals for our mental development. Every Christian should work at becoming a well-rounded individual, continually striving to develop his or her mental capabilities. Failure to set mental goals may lead to religious bigotry, but this can be avoided by reading significant books and deliberately meeting other people and exchanging ideas. Formal education is important, but special emphasis must be placed on reading Christian books with daily attention given to the Bible. By reading the Bible more, we'll get to know Christ better. In Matthew 6:33 we read, "But seek ye first the kingdom of God, and his righteousness; and all these things shall be added unto you." Remember, except for the books you read and the people you meet you'll be the same person five years from now that you are today.

In addition to setting goals for formal education and biblical instruction, we must also continue to shoot for mind-expanding projects. For example, it is possible to become an authority on any subject. To do this just try studying that subject *one hour a day, five days a week, for the next five years*. Since total world knowledge is doubling every five years, it is impossible to keep pace intellectually without some kind of study goals. From 2 Timothy 2:15 we have this advice: "Study to show thyself approved unto God, a workman that needeth not to be ashamed, rightly dividing the word of truth."

At the University of Pennsylvania, there's a little plaque on a wall which reads: "God gave us two ends—one to think with, and one to sit with. All the failure or success in life depends on which end you use. Heads, you win; tails, you lose." It's necessary to set specific mental goals in order to "be ready always to give an answer to every man that asketh you reason of the hope that is in you . . ." (1 Pet. 3:15). Can you give an answer for the hope that is in you? Do you know why you believe? Continue to hone your mind so that it is a credit to God.

Specific Spiritual Goals

To become what we desire, we must set spiritual goals for ourselves. Everything I look at makes me think of God. Elizabeth Barrett Browning said, "Earth is crammed with God." Every bush, tree, and bird talks of God. All creation speaks of the Creator. If we look *out*, we see from eyes that are fantastic. They see in three dimensions and living color. It is beautiful beyond belief. No man could ever make even one of those trees, nor the eyes with which we see.

When we look *back*, we see God moving in history. There is a whole theological study known as "Holy History." The flow of history clearly shows the hand of God. The rise and fall of empires seem to hinge on their moral and spiritual strength more than their military.

When we look *up*, we see the stars. We now know that there are at least eight billion galaxies in outer space, and there are billions of stars in every galaxy. We can set our watches with absolute accuracy by their movement. The exact, precise position of any star in the universe is absolutely predictable. It won't vary a quarter of a second in a hundred years. A recently discovered star in a distant galaxy is so big that the diameter of it is three times greater than the distance between here and the sun, and that is ninety-three million miles. Down in Texas we'd say, "That's an awful big star." We live in a universe that is so big it staggers the imagination just to think about it.

The most elemental laws of science and logic say that there must be a sufficient cause for that which is. If there is a building, there must be a cause for that building. It would be difficult for me to convince you that a building is the result of an accidental collision of building materials in a recent tornado. If I were to try to tell you that, you would laugh because you know that is insufficient cause, and it is illogical and absurd to say. If I see a car sitting by a curb, I know there must be a sufficient cause for that car. You could not convince me that it is the result of an accidental collision of metals. If I see a watch, I know there must be sufficient cause for that watch. It is not the result of an accidental collision of tiny pieces of metal. When I see a universe, I know that there must be a sufficient cause for that universe.

In the university I attended, I had a geology professor who said, "Several hundred billion years ago, there was a collision of heavenly bodies that produced fragments. Those fragments, over a gradual evolutionary process, have become our solar system." And just because our professor said it, we all nodded our heads in unison. (As we did, you could hear the rocks roll around.) Think about how absurd it would be to say that if there was a collision of two automobiles, the result would be a bunch of little automobiles. How ridiculous to think such a thing! When two cars hit, all you have is a wreck! You can introduce all the evolutionary time you like, but when two cars hit, you still have a wreck. Across the hall in the physics department of the same university, I had another professor who said over and over,

"Systems when left to themselves tend to a maximum state of disorder; systems when left to themselves tend to run down." Now get this. The professor across the hall says they don't run down, but that they regulate themselves. This one says they run down and get less orderly. Someone is confused, and I have a sneaking suspicion it isn't God!

There must be sufficient cause for a building. Otherwise, I can make no sense of it. There must be sufficient cause for a car. There must be sufficient cause for a universe with eight billion galaxies and billions of stars in each one. When I look up to the heavens, I have to say this cause is "God!" If I don't say "God," then I am pressed into an absurd, stupid position.

If I look *in*, I see God. Pascal said, "There is a God-shaped vacuum in every heart that can only be filled with Him." The Scripture says in Psalm 42:1, "As the hart [deer] panteth after the water brooks, so panteth my soul after thee, O God." Nothing in this round world can satisfy the triangle-like hunger of my soul for God the *Father, Son,* and *Holy Spirit.* The image of God is stamped by the Creator deep within each of us. Somehow I feel undone and frustrated until I find God. There is no genuine rest, until "we rest in Thee."

In my prison ministry I have often talked to some of the most notorious criminals known to man. But I've never talked to a man or woman that I thought had totally destroyed the image of God within; though at times, it is well concealed. Just a little scratching and there's a telltale sign of guilt, conscience, sense of right and wrong, or even a slight nausea from the stench of his or her own sin.

I still believe in *original sin*—the depravity of man. But I also believe in *original splendor.* We were created for the stars and not for the mud. I've noticed that the inmates always seem to look beyond the prison bars to gaze out at the *stars.*

The image of God within us is never satisfied groveling in the mud of sin or even mediocrity. Man is always reaching out and up toward God. He feels an inner urge to accomplish something of eternal worth and ultimate value. He's like a sick man with a fever, turning and tossing, not finding any comfortable position. Original splendor makes man stretch to fulfill his God-image, the inner fabric of creation.

If I look *up*, I see God. If I look *back*, I see Holy History (God). If I look *out*, I see changing seasons and the beauty and orderliness of this earth (God). If I look *in*, I see a hunger for God. He's everywhere!

Balanced Growth

Luke 2:52 says, "And Jesus increased in wisdom and stature, and in favor with God and man." Christ grew physically, mentally, and spiritually. He was a well-rounded person. Few people I've met in my life have been able to keep a balance of development in all three areas. But this is the great ideal that Christ has set for us!

The body builder flexes proudly and forgets to develop his brain. The student smiles patronizingly at a simplistic statement by a physical extremist, then gives him a verbal jab that would make a slap in the face seem kind. The religionist pulls his self-righteous robes about himself in utter contempt of both. Again, as Christ grew in all areas, so must we.

Man's Search for Meaning

Victor Frankl in *Man's Search for Meaning* said that as a psychologist, he had followed the thinking of Freud. He was therefore amazed at his experience in a World War II concentration camp of Hitler. He saw his fellow inmates starved and stripped of all the comforts of life. They were tortured beyond belief. Most of them died.

Freud had said that men would revert to a base animalistic state when subjected to these conditions. They would tend to react with a sameness. But on the contrary, Frankl discovered that they started to be motivated by "meaning." If they had a strong love, a goal to accomplish, or even hate, then they had a reason to live, and they would survive. They refused to die, being carried outside of themselves by a goal bigger than themselves. They acted more nobly.

Introduce the most horrible tension and it only seems to increase the intensity. Is tension good or bad? It can be either! Frankl says that we don't need a tension-free status, but meaning. We need a goal burned into our beings around which all of life revolves.

The Trap Play

You say, "Okay, Bill, enough of philosophy. How did it all begin with you?" I was just sixteen years old in high school, when I came face to face with Jesus Christ, and he said to me, "I am the way, the truth, and the life: no man cometh unto the Father, but by me." It was like playing defensive end for the Cleveland Browns. When I would charge across the defensive line, usually someone would hit me. Every once in awhile, though, I would charge across the defensive line, and something unique would happen. No one would hit me! Right away, I knew something was wrong because they didn't let me cross that line just to be nice. They didn't let me cross the line so I could clobber their quarterback and throw him for a loss. They let me cross the line so I would think I was going to get a free shot at their quarterback, and then they were going to hit me from the blind side. Sure enough, I would look down to the inside, and here he'd come, charging at me, weighing about 270, and about three feet away. His teeth were gritted, and his head was wagging from side to side. I got the distinct impression that he intended to do me no good! If I did what I really wanted to do, I wouldn't face that big brute head-on. I would sidestep him to the outside, but if I did that, he would bump me out a little further, and the back would cut to the inside and they would make a lot of yards. On the other hand, I could side-step him to the inside, but if I did that, he would turn me in and the back would cut to the outside, and again they would make a lot of yards. The only thing I could do is exactly what I didn't want to do, face that big guard head-on, right in the middle. Now, that's not comfortable, and it's bone-shaking and traumatic. But if I was going to stop him, that was the only way I could do it. This was precisely the way it was for me when I was introduced to Jesus Christ in high school. He said to me, "I am the Way, the Truth, and the Life, and no man gets to God but by Me." I wanted to say, "Sir, you don't understand. I'm a pretty good fellow. I'll turn over a new leaf and I'll get better. I'll go to church two, three, or even four times a year, if you would like. I'll try to do better morally." But I knew that as good as church is, and as good as goodness is, if it is substituted for a relationship with Christ, it has a terrible way of degenerating into self-righteousness, and so I had to face him openly and honestly. I had to say either, "Jesus Christ, you're the biggest liar that ever lived," or, "You are the Son of God, and you're the only possible way to get to God." He is either one, or the other. You say, "I wouldn't say that Jesus Christ is a liar. In fact, I think he was a pretty good man. I don't know that he was the Son of God, but he was certainly a good man and a good example." Don't give me that patronizing garbage. Either Jesus Christ was what he said he was, the Son of God and the only way to get to God, or he was the biggest liar that ever lived. When we are confronted with him, we have to make a decision. Is he the Son of God and the only way to God, or is he just a liar? I discovered that he was exactly what he claimed to be! He will do what he claimed to be able to do. And he claimed to be able to forgive us. He said he would come into our hearts and lives and make us over again. That day, I bowed myself before him, and I crowned him king of my life. I said, "Your way will be my way, and your cause will be my cause; I will follow you all the days of my life."

I challenge you to face Christ openly and honestly, crown him king, and follow him with your whole heart, or walk away from him and call him a big liar. But don't keep riding the fence! He will do what he claimed to be able to do. Don't try to side-step him because if you do, you simply side-step right into your own destruction. Decide what you really want to be spiritually, and be specific. Then "press on toward the goal for the prize of the upward call of God in Jesus Christ" (Phil. 3:14, RSV).

We have discussed the great power of being specific and well-rounded. One other thing may be even more important, and that is to "shoot high." Make your goals big and exciting.

Dr. Carl Bates once said:

> There came a time in my life when I earnestly prayed,
>   "God, I want your power!"
> Time wore on and the power did not come.
>   One day the burden was more than I could bear.
> "God, why haven't You answered that prayer?"
>   God seemed to whisper back His simple reply,
> "With plans no bigger than yours, you don't need My Power."

Some years ago a headline told of the death of three hundred whales. The article went on to tell that the whales had been pursuing sardines when they found themselves marooned in a bay. The small fish had lured the sea giants to their deaths. But the whales had killed themselves by prostituting their vast powers for insignificant goals.

Ask yourself these questions: What are my goals? Are they worthy, important, and well-balanced? Remember, big goals create great excitement!

Ways to Make This Step on the Ladder Work

1. Begin to picture the aimed-for goal as if it were a reality.

2. In addition to writing down your specific goals, begin to talk about them. If it's not wise to share it with others, talk to yourself.

3. Choose friends who will help you achieve your goals. Now

obviously, you as a Christian can't afford to avoid people who could never help you. But you must cultivate some close friends who can.

4. Picture in vivid detail what you want to do. Hold it intensely in your mind until it is marked there as if it were indelibly imprinted. It is filed there like a computer tape and can be triggered into action at will.

5. Double your effort. Like the financier, Bernard Baruch, said, "Decide what you really want, then decide what you're willing to pay to achieve it." Are you willing to do twice what's expected of you?

6. Some people keep waiting for their ship to come in, but they never sent one out! Or what's worse, they sent one out and weren't aware of it. It was laden with negative failure pictures. When it comes back (and it will) the negative pictures will have multiplied. Likewise, if we send out positive pictures they come back *multiplied!*

7. We all tend to be disciplined in the area of our strength. So it is easy to come up with clear, specific goals. I challenge you to do what's tough. Try to set goals and aggressively pursue them in the areas of your weakness.

8. On a three-by-five inch index card, write simple, clear, specific goals for all three areas of your life—physical, mental, and spiritual. Include on the card the date that you visualize the projected victory. Get the card duplicated and put one in your shirt pocket or in your purse. Put one on your mirror, desk, and the instrument panel of your car. Hold a mental picture of what you have written. Give it all you've got and believe that God will help you attain your goal. Remember, we move toward our goals like heat-seeking missiles. That's why you must have clear goals.

9. Set high, worthy, and important goals. Dream great dreams!

There is creative power in clearly-defined, realistic goals, dated, and positively determined goals. But in addition to this, hang in there when it is tough, work hard, pray humbly to God, and know your goals are reachable within the time limit!

4.

TAKE RESPONSIBILITY

The Fourth Rung of the Ladder Is to Be Responsible

In the final seconds, a great receiver speeds down the sidelines, and catches the pass that wins the game. The defensive back that was supposed to cover him is embarrassed before fifty million people on national television. What does he do? Does he come back to the huddle and apologize to the defensive linemen who have been breaking their necks to get to the quarterback? No. He comes back to the huddle dragging his leg. All the spectators say, "Poor guy. He has a pulled muscle. No wonder he missed the coverage." This is what a friend of mine calls the "Loser's Limp." It's the player's excuse for not doing his job.

Side-stepping Started with Adam and Eve

It started in the Garden of Eden. God said in essence to Adam, "Was that you I saw eating the fruit of the Tree of Life?" Adam said, "It was that woman you gave me. She tempted me to do it!" Men have always tried to blame women for their sins. But Adam even went a step further. By blaming the woman that "*you* gave me," he was in fact saying, "You should have known better than that, God. You should have known that woman was going to do that to me, so in reality, it's your fault."

So God turned to Eve and said, "Did you tempt Adam?" She said, "It was the Devil that made me do it. He's the one that tempted me!" People usually shift the blame to someone else. Comedian Flip Wilson wasn't the first one to blame the Devil for his sin. People today blame everything and everyone for their sin but themselves. Luck, fate, the horoscope, the government, Satan, timing, predestination, everything, and everyone on earth is blamed except ourselves. There is nothing more basic to the sin nature than blaming others.

God runs the universe, but I am free enough to be responsible and accountable. I have no patience with any theology that cuts out my own personal accountability. Recently I was talking with a man who was doing something that I considered to be wrong. He assured me that he was certain God wouldn't allow him to do anything that would hurt the cause of Christ. However, he would not agree to stop doing the thing which was wrong. Somehow, he had disassociated himself from responsibility. In other words, "I don't intend to change, but I am certain that God will work it out so that what I'm doing won't hurt anything or anybody."

The Bible Teaches Personal Responsibility

It is possible to be so preoccupied with a "Christ-in-you" philosophy that we feel totally absolved of any responsibility. I'd be the last to be critical of the Spirit-filled life. It is only the phony version of it that plays a game with words and omits blame or credit that I criticize. In Romans 14:12 we read, "Every man must give an account of *himself* before God." So the Bible forces us back to personal responsibility.

In 2 Samuel 12:7 Nathan, the prophet of God, stands before David with eyes wide open and boldly says, "Thou art the man!" Pointing his bony finger in David's face he accuses him of adultery and murder.

I once read of a southern governor who visited the state penitentiary, and while walking through the institution, he was approached by numerous inmates. The first blamed his crime on his parents. The second assured the governor that the judge was against him. The third laid it on his lawyer. The fourth accused society. The fifth complained about the prison conditions and bad administration within the prison. One after another the inmates shifted the blame to everyone and everything but themselves. Finally, just before he left the institution, one inmate came up to him and said, "You know, I really deserve to be here. I was caught committing a really serious crime and I deserve to be in this prison." When the governor got back to his mansion, he wrote a letter to the warden. He said, "I want you to get that last man I talked to out of the prison as soon as possible. I don't want him contaminating all those 'innocent people' you have there in the penitentiary. I am enclosing a pardon for him, so release him immediately!" It is extremely difficult to bring prison inmates to the point where they will face up to personal responsibility for their own actions. When one is able to do that, there is hope. It is certain that as long as the inmate is blaming someone else, he can never find a solution to his problem. But this is not unique or surprising, because it is also true of every one of us.

After the resurrection, our Lord took a seaside walk with Peter, encouraging him to "follow me" and be the leader of the whole Christian movement. Turning and seeing John following at a distance, Peter said, "But Lord, what about John?" And the Lord said, "Never mind John, I'm talking to you, Peter."

It is great to give God the credit for all the good things that happen in our lives and Satan the blame for that which is bad. However, this must not ever be used as a way to dodge responsibility. So many of us are falling into the trap of blaming the environment when things go wrong. No doubt, our backgrounds do have great impact on our actions. However, we're free to choose our own reactions to those influences. We're free to choose our own attitudes. So we would be much better off not to blame our childhood, God, luck, fate, the horoscope, or anything else, but rather to take responsibility for ourselves.

Taking the Credit and the Blame for What We Do

Begin to take credit and blame for everything that happens in your life. Don't say, "I had to work late." Say, "I chose to work late." Don't complain, "I had to practice football today," but, "I chose to practice football." Don't say, "I had to pick up my child after school," but "I chose to pick up my child after school."

Maybe you have the wrong idea about humility. You think that humility is *degrading* yourself. Actually, the humble person is the one who is so wrapped up in what he is doing that he never thinks of himself, but only of the goal he is trying to accomplish. But if self should cross his mind, there is a great sense of self-respect because self is made in the image of God by God. And it has great innate worth.

I must give an account of myself before God. But the "I" is drained of pride and filled with responsibility. Obviously, if we over-glorify ourselves for that which is good in our lives, we are guilty of the sin of self-righteousness and pride. However, there is a healthy assumption of responsibility that fills the "I" with a sense of duty, rather than arrogance.

Why Do People Continue to Do Evil?

I was recently on a plane and a lovely elderly black lady sat beside me. As we flew above the clouds, she was reading her Bible. I started a conversation with her, and when she discovered that I was a minister, she said there was something bothering her. She said, "You know, the people in my neighborhood do bad things, and it always seems to hurt them. Why do they keep doing bad things when it eventually is going to hurt them?" I showed her in her Bible the verse in Ecclesiastes 8:11, which says, "Because sentence against an evil work is not executed speedily, therefore the heart of the sons of men is fully set in them to do evil." Why do men continue to do evil? Because judgment is not always executed speedily. If someone reached out to take something that wasn't his, and a divine ax came out of heaven and chopped his hand off, it might discourage him from stealing. If there was immediate, just judgment the instant anyone committed a robbery, there would be very little stealing. If every time we told a lie, a divine baseball bat came out of heaven and knocked our teeth out, it would discourage lying. However, because judgment is not executed speedily, people may come to the conclusion that it will not be executed at all. This is a foolish conclusion. God is simply giving us a space or delayed time frame in which to repent.

Don't misinterpret his longsuffering and patience with the foolish conclusion that he will not execute judgment. The fact is, he *will* judge everyone!

Not long ago I was stopped by a policeman for speeding and had to go to court. I faced a woman judge. Reading from the record, she discovered that I was a minister. Very cynically, she said, "Reverend, do you want justice?" I replied, "No ma'am, I want mercy!" When I stand before God, I don't want justice, for if I got justice, I would be chopped in half. What I want is mercy! When you stand before God, you can be certain that what is noble and right will be approved, and what is base and wrong will be disapproved. However, God will deal with us according to his mercy and grace, and not in strict accord with what we really deserve.

You Are In Control

God has given us the freedom and responsibility to control our own lives. We really can't get rid of ourselves, not even by committing suicide. Because if we do commit suicide, when it is over, we are still wherever we are. And we really haven't gotten ourselves off our hands; we have only changed our location. It is not our circumstances that need changing. We need changing! Jesus Christ is the only one who has the power to do that. However, he will only help if we face up to our personal responsibility.

There is really no duty without responsibility. If a person won't take responsibility for his actions, then he feels no sense of duty to get anything accomplished. Remember, you are in control, and the decisions you make affect the destiny of your life.

Turn Potential into Reality

We are what we are by the composite of all the decisions we have made in the past. The rewards that we have in this life and in the life to come are in direct relationship to the service we have rendered. I don't mean by this idea to disavow grace. There is much which we get in this world, and in the one to come, that is totally undeserved. But even those gifts aren't crammed down our throats. We must put ourselves in position to receive them by repentance, faith, obedience, and prayer.

Coach Vince Lombardi used to say, "Potential means you ain't done it yet." We must turn our potentials into realities. We can't afford to leave them to chance. We each determine the direction of our lives—we are the ones behind the wheel. We are doing the driving. And we must assume personal responsibility for our actions.

The Bible teaches cause and effect. If you give generously, you get wealth in return. I used to think that the Christian should give with no thought of getting anything in return. I still think that is a noble ideal, but not scriptural. In Luke 6:38, we read, "give, and it will be given to you; good measure, pressed down, shaken together, running over, will be put into your lap. For the measure you give, will be the measure you get back" (RSV). "Give and it will be given to you" is consistent with Bible teaching. In fact, there is hardly a passage on giving anywhere in the Bible that doesn't teach this. It even goes further to say that our return will be in proportion to our giving. "For

the measure you give, will be the measure you get back."
This is also true of service. Ideally, we should follow Christ
because we love him. But he said in Matthew 19:29, "And every
one that hath forsaken houses, or brethren, or sisters, or father,
or mother, or wife, or children, or lands, for my name's sake,
shall receive a hundredfold, and shall inherit everlasting life."
If we follow him, he promises that in this life and in the life
to come we will "receive a hundredfold and inherit everlasting
life." During life on earth or in heaven, we'll be paid back a
hundred times over. And even the bad that comes will work
out to our own good, according to Romans 8:28.

If we plant wisely, we will reap great good. If we take control
of our own bodies, our own spirits, and our own souls, we can
move out in God's strength to accomplish great things. Losers
"let" it happen; winners "make" it happen. God rewards bold
aggressive action in his service. But we must act responsibly to
turn our potentials into the realities God intended. "Whatsoever
thy hand findeth to do, do it with thy might" (Eccles. 9:10).

One of our prison counselors was aboard a plane on his way
to a prison crusade not long ago. The man sitting next to him
asked where he was going. The counselor said, "To a prison to
work with the Bill Glass Team. We live with the inmates in
prison for three days and try to help them spiritually and otherwise." The man said, "Don't you really think that is sort of a
lost cause? Those inmates can't really change. You can't change
the leopard's spots, and you can't change a bunch of cons into
decent citizens." The counselor said, "I don't know. My name
is Nick the Greek. I spent four years in prison, and I have
been out over four years now. That entire time I've been working
in the rehabilitation of inmates through Jesus Christ. I know
that I will never go back to a life of crime, and I believe there
has been a total change in my life."

Nick didn't leave the development of his potential to chance.
He took responsibility for his actions, and he chose to change
his life. His decision to follow Christ was the first step to a
new life.

Reality Therapy

Psychologists are discovering that good mental health comes from right relationships with God and man. They are finding that what God said in his Word is just good, common-sense living.

William Glasser's book, *Reality Therapy*, (Harper & Row, Publishers, Inc., 1965) simply says that we all have two basic needs: (1) to love and be loved, and (2) to feel that we are worthwhile to ourselves and to others.

Glasser also places a great deal of importance on responsibility. Dispensing with common psychiatric labels such as *neurosis* and *psychosis*, he replaces them with responsibility. If someone is mentally ill, in most cases, he has simply been acting irresponsibly. He has been pursuing his basic needs of love and meaning in unrealistic or irresponsible ways. So, it is the task of the psychologist to help the person fulfill his needs in responsible ways, which is exactly the position of the Bible. Man is responsible and accountable and will be better off in this life and the next if he faces up to it. Good mental health is simply good Christianity.

Happiness comes when we are willing to take responsibility for our behavior. Irresponsible people are always seeking to gain happiness without assuming responsibility. They find only brief periods of joy, but not the deep-seated satisfaction which accompanies responsible lifestyle. They often try to avoid responsibility through alcohol, drugs, casual sex, or other side-stepping maneuvers. The true friend, like a good parent, needs to try to help the suffering person face reality and admit his need for responsible action. Don't allow him to blame others or justify himself; for in so doing, he is avoiding reality.

Human nature can change, so long as we face our sins and our needs responsibly. Man always attempts to cover up his sin, but Proverbs 28:13 says, "He that covereth his sins shall not prosper; but whoso confesseth and forsaketh them shall have mercy." We must confess and forsake our sins if we are ever to be right with God. We must take control of all areas of our lives and not let circumstances or anything but God guide us.

How to Make This Step on the Ladder Work

Here are several suggestions that can help you face up to your responsibilities:

1. Take control of your life by facing, confessing, and forsaking your sin.

2. Take control of your thoughts. Given enough time, our dominant thoughts become acts. The victory comes when we never allow negative or sinful thoughts to dominate our minds. In the Sermon on the Mount, Jesus teaches us the importance of the thought-controlled life.

3. Remember that you have the freedom to choose, and the way you choose will shape your destiny. Know where you are going. Remember, you are in the driver's seat. The decisions you make will affect your life.

4. Pray without ceasing. This is asking God's presence, power, and strength within your life, but never relinquishing your accountability.

5. Remember, the worst sin is to blame the environment for your failures. Instead of blaming others, take responsibility for your own actions. In other words, say, "By the choices that I make, I am the cause of the results that happen in my life." If you stop living responsibly, you will lose touch with reality and your mental health will be affected.

6. Study to show yourself approved, a workman that need not be ashamed. Study and work, and be approved by God.

7. Cut the words *I can't* and *I had to* out of your vocabulary.

8. Don't leave the development of your potential to chance. Take control of your life.

9. Compliment your child when he makes a wise choice. Praise only the things in your children and others for which they are responsible and can change—things such as character traits. Say, for example, "You have such a good attitude."

Theology or ideology that dodges personal responsibility can soon become disenchanting. As long as we are giving God the credit line, we have taken another step up the ladder to successful Christian living. But when we start blaming God for either our sins, our laziness, or our sloppiness, that's side-stepping and covering up.

The Statue of Liberty in New York Harbor reminds us that we are all free. But we need to place a Statue of Responsibility in San Francisco Bay to remind us that because of our freedom, both nationally and individually, we are also responsible and will give an account of every deed and word done in the flesh.

5.

CHOOSE REAL FRIENDS

The Fifth Rung of the Ladder Is to Seek Good Friends

God has made us such that we love friends. In fact, we can't really get along very well without them. We don't mature into the kind of individuals we ought to be unless we have friends. They are like paintings. When a great painting is put in good light, the effect will be excellent. But, when the same painting is put in bad light, the effect is ruined. Friends bring out the very best in us, just as proper lighting brings out the best in paintings. Friends challenge us, listen to us, and help us. We can't get along without them.

Robert Stroud killed two men and, as a result, was put in an island prison called Alcatraz, which was in the middle of San Francisco Bay. He was left there for thirty years. He had no human contact for those years, so he made canaries into confidantes, and lovers out of larks. He became the "Bird Man of Alcatraz." Why did he do this? Because within every one of us there is a need for contact with other living things. Ideally, it should be with other people. But, if not with humans, at least with other things that are alive and breathing—even if it must be a bird!

Confession Is Important

Ministers are no different than lay people. We all have problems, and we need to share them with others. Unless we have someone to share our problems with, we cannot grow into the kind of individuals we ought to be. Protestantism has come so far away from the Catholic confessional that we have forgotten one of the prime teachings of the New Testament, "Confess your faults one to another, and pray one for another, that ye may be healed" (James 5:16). Now, I don't believe you can forgive me, but I believe it is highly therapeutic and highly strengthening to confess to someone. In order to share problems, we must have someone we can trust. In fact, if we don't have someone like that, we can't grow as we ought. Just as this passage in James states, confession to friends promotes healing.

Two Things We Need from Others

There are two important things about friends: I need you and I need to be needed by you.

Sometime ago, the wife of the mayor of San Francisco disappeared. No one knew where she was. She just vanished. After eighteen days, Mayor Alioto's wife finally came back and a big press conference was called. She was asked, "Where were you and why did you leave?" She said, "Well, my daughter found a wonderful young man and she got married. They have a very happy marriage. Of course, I'm very happy for her, but she no longer needed me. My husband decided to run for Governor of California, and he didn't even confer with me. Obviously, I assumed he didn't need me. Nobody needed me, so I just ran away." And there she stood, one of the richest women in all of California in her elegant dress, beautiful jewelry, and lovely home—the mayor's wife—and she was saying, "I'm miserable because nobody needs me." She stood there like a little girl, saying, "Nobody loves me or wants me." She was merely articulating a deep human need, one that we all share because every one of us needs to be needed—"I need you, and I need to be needed by you."

Finding friends with whom we can share our problems and our victories is an important Christian concept.

We need a symbiotic relationship with others. Have you ever seen African movies in which there was a rhino with a tick bird on its back? The tick bird dearly loves to eat the insects that crawl in and out of the folds of fat around the rhino's neck, and the rhino enjoys having all those insects eaten out by the tick bird. What if you were a rhino and you had no one to eat the insects out of the folds of fat around your neck? Life would be miserable! The tick bird needs the rhino for food and transportation. The rhino needs the tick bird for disinfection. That's a symbiotic relationship.

Another type of relationship is called a parasitic relationship. It's like moss hanging on a tree. The moss sucks all its food from the tree and gives nothing in return. This is an unhealthy relationship. But, a symbiotic relationship is beneficial to both individuals. The tick bird strengthens the rhino, and the rhino feeds the tick bird. They really need each other. We're like that, aren't we? We really need each other. We need friends that we trust enough to share our worst defeats and our greatest victories.

Someone with Whom to Share Victories

You may have heard of the minister who had a secret desire to play golf on Sunday mornings. Well, he could never get rid of it! He always wanted to play golf on Sunday morning. Members of his church talked of playing golf on Sunday mornings, but he never could. Finally, it just overwhelmed him. He got his associate to preach for him, and he went to play golf one Sunday morning. He felt guilty about it; nevertheless, he played. He was doing pretty well when Saint Peter looked down from heaven and saw this wicked, golf-playing preacher. He said to Michael, the Archangel, who was standing nearby, "Watch me. I'm gonna fix him." About that time, the parson was making a drive. Saint Peter crooked his finger at the ball. It went about three hundred yards in the air, hit in a drainage ditch, rolled down the ditch, through a drainpipe, across the fairway, through a sandtrap, across the green, and into the hole. A hole in one!

"What kind of punishment is that? You let him make the hole in one!" said Michael. "Oh," Peter said, "that's the worst kind of punishment. Who's he gonna tell?" And that *is* a terrible punishment, isn't it? For unless we have someone with whom we can share our victories, they're like sawdust in our mouths. Unless we have someone with whom to share our problems, they can destroy us. But, if we have someone with whom we can share those problems and victories, we have a treasure. We have a real friend. Without such friends we'll be immature, powerless, lopsided and weak.

"Rejoice with them that do rejoice, and weep with them that weep" (Rom. 12:15). I find that there are a lot of people I trust enough to share my problems with, but there are very few I feel close enough to, to share my victories with. It takes a much better friend to share victories than to share problems. I guess the reason is viewpoint. If we are sharing problems with friends, they are looking down on us and giving us their sympathy and understanding. If we are sharing our victories, they are looking up to us. It's much easier to look down on people than it is to look up to them!

Evil Men Make Bad Friends

Just as friends are imperative, they are also dangerous. Friends can get too close to us. And we get to trusting them so much that we allow them to influence us to do things we would not otherwise do. In 1 Samuel 13, we read about Amnon, the son of David, who had an evil friend by the name of Jonadab. It was Jonadab who thought up the whole wicked plot to rape Tamar. It never occurred to Amnon. One would think Amnon would listen to the voice of conscience, which said, "Don't take advantage of this poor, helpless little girl. You are a powerful, strong man!" But, Amnon wasn't listening to the voice of conscience. He was listening to his "friend" Jonadab. You would think he'd listen to the voice of reason: "No man ever thought up sex. It was made by God. He knows us. He best understands us. There would be no real joy in forced sex. He knows those rules by which we operate best." But, he wasn't listening to reason. He was listening to the voice of his "friend." One would think he would listen to the voice of God, who, in essence, has said, "one man for one woman for life." But he wasn't listening to the voice of God. He was listening to the voice of Jonadab. One would think he would listen to the voice of his father. David was king of all the land. Such a proud family—a family who was supposed to be the moral leader of the nation. Would he not listen to his father? No, he was listening to his "friend," Jonadab.

Evil men make bad friends. But, we live in a day in which it's not popular to call anyone evil, for we're not supposed to be so judgmental. However, from most plays and movies seen on television, one would think that bartenders are a person's best friends and prostitutes are the only ones who are nonjudgmental. They'll listen to your problems. The plots always seem to portray ministers, policemen, and judges as individuals who want to keep us from having a good time by telling us "No, no, no." But God has said, "one man for one woman for life," (taught clearly in Matt. 5:32, 19:6; Rom. 7:2–3) because he knows that's the only thing that will really work. Now we might not live up to that divine ideal, but when we don't, God's forgiveness is always available. We simply have to ask for it. But don't ever think that God doesn't know what he's talking about.

Roger Staubach says, "If loving my wife and being faithful to her and my children is being square, then call me a square." I think Roger Staubach has a better sexual adjustment and relationship and is happier than the playboy type, who brags about his sexual freedom. Why? Because Roger's done it God's way.

Parents have been tongue-tied, and ministers have been timid. We need a whole new generation of pastors and lay people who have the guts to say, "Thus saith the Lord!" If we don't, then we're in trouble, because our young people will continue to drift, not knowing what is right and wrong, what is good and bad.

Watergate

Wasn't that the case in Watergate? In a conversation with Chuck Colson in which we discussed Watergate, he told me, "If there had been just one Christian who would have stood up and said, 'What is right, gentlemen?' it probably would never have taken place. But, no one had the courage to ask that." They were saying, "What's gonna work? What can we get away with? You are the President of the United States! Can't you make up your own mind about good and bad? Haven't other presidents done these same things?" "What's right" was never considered. The reason we had this great scandal was because there was no one to say, "Thus saith the Lord." No one said, "What does God say about it?" And there were all types of rationalizations.

My own son, Bobby, was just 15 years old when he was approached by one of his friends who told him how he should keep an open mind to the possible use of drugs. Bobby told me what his friend said, and I warned him, "You know, this guy you're talking about sounds like a pusher." Bobby said, "Oh, no, Dad. He's not a pusher. He's a real nice guy. He never even uses drugs himself. He just wants me to keep an open mind. He says it's mind expanding. He's not even suggesting I should use them. He just says I should stay open." Three days later that young friend of Bobby's hit a telephone pole going 70 miles per hour on a motorcycle. It killed him instantly. After the accident, a large amount of drugs was discovered in his home. He was one of the biggest pushers in town—and he was trying to cut my son's guts out! He was a Jonadab—posing to be a friend, but not really a friend at all. Evil men make bad friends.

I was in a church several years ago, and a group of young people were talking to me. They were saying how beautiful and sweet *Love Story* was. I said, "Do you realize that our Lord's name was used in vain twenty-three different times in the movie *Love Story?* Both lead characters are agnostic or atheistic, and they're participating in premarital sex unashamedly? Most of what the movie *Love Story* stands for morally, God stands against. Just because they're wrapped with a little tear-jerking doesn't make premarital sex, using the Lord's name in vain, and atheism correct. They're still dead wrong!" Christian young people and adults must be more intelligent than that.

The Devil Gives His Best First

In John 2:10, we read that, contrary to custom, the best wine was served last at the wedding feast in Cana. This was possible because of the miracle Jesus performed. This is characteristic of him. He always saves the best until last. Remember how Paul, on the Damascus Road, ran head-on into a blinding light and was struck blind for three days? He stumbled in a stupor. It was a bitter thing for him to admit his sin and repent. He had to admit that he'd been wrong in his persecution of Christians, but he soon began to experience great things with God, and his reward was eternal life.

It is the reverse with Satan. He always gives us his best first. But, it isn't long until it takes more and more to get the same kick, and we're hooked. The alcohol is warm and freeing to the personality at first, but it takes an increasing amount to get the same glow, and finally, we're hooked! The stolen sex thrill is warm and wonderful at first, but it is counterfeit love. It ends in enslavement. Satan always gives us the best shot first, but it gets worse as it goes and ends in hell. There is a diminishing return. It takes more and more to get the same kick out of sin.

Don't Buy the Lie

Too many people buy the lie that sin is fun, and it will get better as it goes. The truth is that it's fun at first, but it gets worse as it goes. It ends in addiction, destruction, and disillusionment.

This is what Paul speaks of when he says, "It was sin, working death in me through what is good, in order that sin might be shown to be sin, and through the commandment might become sinful beyond measure" (Rom. 7:13, RSV). If we could see sin as it really is—deception and a big lie!—and could hear the death rattle in the music of this world, then we would not be so easily deceived by the Jonadabs. The wages of sin are indeed death! (Rom. 6:23).

High School Survey

In a survey in schools across America ten young men and women were taken into a class. Nine of the ten were told to lie about the length of two lines to be drawn on the chalkboard. The tenth student was not in on the secret. The teacher would tell him to draw two lines on the chalkboard; she would point to the obviously shorter line and say, "How many of you think this is the longest line?" Nine hands would go up. The tenth one in the room, who hadn't been informed, would look around and see all the others with their hands up, so he'd put his up. The teacher would point to the other line with the question "How many think this is the shortest line?" and nine hands would go up. The tenth student could see that it was obviously wrong, but because everyone else's hand was up, he didn't want to appear to be a fool. So, he'd put his hand up. In 85 percent of the cases in surveys all over America, the tenth one would go along with the other nine. And what do you think happens in a beer bust, a pot-smoking party, or a sex orgy? The pressure is on to smoke pot, to drink, and to be sexually promiscuous because "everyone else" is doing it. But God says, "Don't go along with the crowd." He says, "Don't listen to the Jonadabs. Do what's right, no matter what!"

Let's look back at 2 Samuel 13 again. Amnon didn't listen to God. He listened to his friend, Jonadab. I would say there is hardly a person alive today who doesn't know a Jonadab or a Delilah. Jonadab isn't always male. One in twenty inmates in prison is a woman. There are Delilahs who would encourage you to take shortcuts with truth. They can manipulate others into doing their meanness for them.

There's hardly a businessman who doesn't know a Jonadab who would say, "Oh, why don't you take the easy way?" The man in politics faces it daily. Certainly ministers face Jonadabs. They're encouraged to do what is expedient, rather than what is right. If you listen to Jonadabs, you die—spiritually and sometimes physically. Evil men make bad friends.

Be gutsy enough to label evil men and women. The evil man is the one who will encourage you to forget the long-term loss, and take the short-term gain. He will tell you to follow your gut rather than your God, your glands rather than your brain. "All right," you say, "I will admit that there are always Jonadabs pressuring me. But how do you defeat Jonadab?"

How to Defeat Jonadab

First, we must cling to our convictions. We must run the banner of what we believe high on the flagpoles of our lives and defend it from any man or woman who would try to pull it down. We must establish our moral position before we ever get into a situation—decide where we stand and hang in there with our whole heart! If we pre-think our position ahead of time, we will certainly not cave in when we get into a pressured situation.

It is important to decide what we believe about illicit sex, dishonesty, drugs, alcohol, and every other temptation. Then, when we get in the pressure situation, we will be victorious. Parents or pastors who are not sure of their position can be assured that those they influence will be weak.

Second, we must cling to our courage. If we stand for God and for his Son, Jesus Christ, there will be a day when we will think we're standing alone. There is hardly a Christian adult or young person who hasn't felt as though he was the only one. We have all thought we were the only ones trying to do the right thing.

My own children have said to me many times, "Dad, I'm the only one! I'm the only one who doesn't smoke pot! I'm the only one who doesn't participate in premarital sex. I'm the only one who doesn't drink." Romans 11:4 says that God answered Elijah (when he complained he was the only one who hadn't bowed the knee to Baal) with, "I have reserved to myself seven thousand men, who have not bowed their knee to the image of Baal." He was saying, "Look, don't get so self-righteous. There are seven thousand others just like you!"

Cling to your courage. If you decide to stand for Jesus Christ, there will come a day when you think you're the only one. It won't be true, but even if it were, it would still be right.

Third, we must understand our enemy. As I was just saying, we must label him an evil man. For he's the one who advises contradictory to God's way. He will give us his best shot first, but it's going to get worse as it goes. We must realize that though sin may be fun at first, there is a diminishing return. Ultimately, our joy turns to pain and destruction!

Fourth, since we're going to be pressured by Jonadab, we must cling to Christ. Proverbs 18:24 says though there are those who pose to be friends, ". . . there is a friend that sticketh closer than a brother." Christ can always be trusted and he alone will give us power to stand!

In summary, I'd like to encourage you to make a list of the attributes you want in a friend. Remember, you want a symbiotic friend, not a parasitic friend—one who strengthens you and one whom you strengthen in return.

You want one with whom you can share your problems and your victories—one who will weep with you when you weep and rejoice with you when you rejoice. One who will share your burdens and your hurts, as well as your victories. Find a friend who knows you well, yet accepts you anyway in spite of your faults. I suppose the greatest example of friendship in the entire Bible is that of Jonathan and David. The Scripture says in 1 Samuel 23:16 that Jonathan strengthened David's hand in God. That's what a true friend does. He forgets his own self-interest and puts genuine, enthusiastic involvement into the life of his friend. He is most concerned to help at the point of our weakness.

The Acid Test for Husbands

One day as I was reading, I received great insight into the practical side of friendship as it relates to family. I came across an account of a woman who had returned from the grocery store. She was explaining to her husband how humiliated she had been. She'd tried to cash a check, and the manager had refused to accept it. He protested that she had been the one who "bounced" a check on him last month and insisted that she follow him to his office to discuss it further. They discovered that the name of the person who had actually bounced the check earlier was similar to hers, but spelled differently. He apologized profusely, but she complained tearfully to her husband how she had felt like dropping through the floor. "Honestly, I was humiliated. Friends were in the line with me and heard him accuse me of bouncing the check. It was awful!" The article continued, "Now how should the husband react?" (1) "Oh, that's unimportant. Those people don't really care that much, and they'll soon forget it." (2) "Well, just explain to your friends or insist that the manager do it for you." (3) "I'm gonna sue him or beat him up!" Or (4) None of the above.

The answer was "None of the above." The right answer was, "I wish I could have been there with you. I know you must have been terribly embarrassed and humiliated."

Most men want to be the problem solvers whose shining armor glistens as they come riding in on their white horses to save the day. It's so easy and self-fulfilling to give a quick answer.

But those close to you—your wife or child or friend—simply want you to know that they are hurting and want you to feel the hurt with them. This came as a flash of insight to me— one of my "Ah ha!" experiences.

The Acid Test for Fathers

After reading the article, I walked out of the study and into my son's bedroom where my wife was standing, hands on hips, in sheer frustration. I asked her, "What's the problem?" The doctors had just called to tell us that Bobby was going to have to go back to the hospital. Eighteen-year-old, 240-pound Bobby was lying on his bed. He had just recently been given a football scholarship to Baylor University. This should have been a great time in his life. He had his head buried in the pillow, crying in frustration. His mother was saying, "We've gotta go to the hospital, Bobby. The doctors insist that we have to go right now." He looked up long enough to beat the pillow and say, "I'm not going to the hospital. I don't care what you say! I'm not going! I've been in the hospital most of the time for the last year and a half, and I refuse to go back. You can't make me!" He was as strong as a bull at six feet, four inches, and I wasn't certain that I was strong enough to make him—plus the fact that I'd just read the article.

My gut reaction was to say, "Come on! Get up from that bed. Don't get discouraged. We're going to the hospital, and we'll get the best doctors in the country. We'll pray about it. We'll lick this thing together!" But, I thought, "Why not try something different?"

So, as he lay on the bed with his head in the pillow, I sat down on the floor beside him. I said nothing for quite awhile. Finally, I broke the silence. "Son, I know how you feel. You've been given this scholarship to play football. You're not certain whether or not you'll be able to play because you have this terrible hip infection which the doctors haven't been able to cure for the last year and a half. You've spent about half of your time in the hospital since then. You hate the hospital. Your hip hurts. You don't think the doctors can help you because they haven't been successful in the past. You're frustrated and unhappy. I don't blame you, because so am I! You feel like giving up. I feel the same way. I know how you feel." My son raised up and looked at me in disbelief because he'd never heard his dad be that negative. Then he put his head back down in the pillow, and I continued with my head drooped in despair. After about two or three minutes of deafening silence, he jumped up on the bed, hit the pillow hard enough to shake the walls of the house, and said, "Come on, Dad. Don't get discouraged. We're going to the hospital, we'll get the best doctors, we'll pray about it, believe God, and we're gonna have a victory in this thing. Come on. Let's go to the hospital."

All he wanted to know was that I understood and that I hurt with him. He didn't need me to solve his problems or come to the right conclusions. He needed a friend to share his hurt.

The Ideal Friend

There is one other thing about this "ideal friend." He must have a positive, faith attitude. He must suggest statements that will build positive pictures in our minds. A friend who has a negative unbelieving attitude tends to program us in the wrong direction. Obviously, the greatest need of all is not to go out seeking an ideal friend like this, but to be that kind of person yourself. Then you'll be swamped with people who will want you as a friend because you are the kind of person whom they've always thought of as friends themselves. Everyone wants a friend like you are becoming!

How to Make This Step on the Ladder Work

1. Seek a friend you trust completely. Share honestly both your problems and your victories. Let the tick bird-rhino relation-

ship remind you of the kind of symbiotic Christian friend you need and need to be.

2. Remember that evil men make bad friends!

3. Be on your guard against Satan. He gives you his best shot first, but it gets worse as it goes along. Then it ends in destruction.

4. Remember how to defeat Jonadab:

(a) Cling to your convictions. Pre-think your moral position on sex, drugs, alcohol, lying, cheating, bigotry, and every potentially tempting situation that may arise. Otherwise, under the pressure of the crowd, you'll be enticed away.

(b) Cling to your courage. You may say, "I'm the only one in my high school who is living a Christian life. I'm the only virgin, nonuser of drugs, etc." This probably isn't true, though you may think it is, but it is still right to stand for God even if you stand alone!

(c) Understand Satan, the enemy. He's trying to get you to "buy the lie" that sin is fun and it's going to get even better.

(d) Cling to Christ! He alone can give you strength to stand.

(e) Don't always try to be the problem solver. Try understanding and hurting with others!

5. Choose friends with a positive attitude toward themselves and others. They will encourage and reinforce pictures of success in your mind.

6. Decide to be the ideal friend. Then you will attract the same kind of friends.

6.

HANDLE YOUR HURTS

The Sixth Rung of the Ladder Is to Learn to Handle Hurts

I remember when I was just a kid, our coach got all of us together. He said, "Men, football is a tough game. In fact, it is a very rough game—so dangerous that sooner or later, you have to expect to get hurt. It is the football player who learns to handle his hurts that will make it." I soon discovered he was right about football. He was also right about life. I've learned that sooner or later, everyone is going to get hurt. You say, "Well, Bill, I've never been hurt." Then you just wait awhile. You will be hurt. The victory goes to that person who learns to handle his hurts.

Nursing Your Hurts

I read about a woman down in Mississippi who had a daughter who died at the age of five. She loved that daughter so desperately she went every day to place freshly-cut flowers on her grave. She drove a total of 110 miles round-trip each day to visit this child's burial place. Her grief was so deep that the other living children left home early, and her husband divorced her. She went stark-raving mad because she simply couldn't handle her hurt. She was "nursing" her hurt.

How many times have you heard people say about a man, "That man has been going downhill ever since he got passed over for a promotion on his job"? Or, "That young woman has been going downhill ever since she was jilted by that man"? A lot of people face terrible problems or hurts, and they just can't help nursing their hurt.

Rehearsing Your Hurts

These people "rehearse" their hurts, constantly talking about them. They do this so much that it becomes self-fulfilling. It is good to "get it out in the open" and honestly admit that we have a problem, but if it is repeated constantly, the reinforcement of the failure pattern is so strong that similar, or even worse things, can occur.

Elvis Presley's mother died at the age of 43. Elvis himself began to be obsessed with the idea that he would die at the same age. He "nursed" the idea, and even "rehearsed" it to his friends. It finally became so strong that it turned into a self-fulfilling prophecy. He died in the same month of the year, at the same age that his mother died.

Don't fail to share your hurts with a trusted friend, but don't overdo it. You'll ruin yourself and run your friends away—or drive them nuts!

Cursing Your Hurts

A lot of inmates I know "curse" their hurts. Because their fathers kicked them around and abused them as children, they have a deep hatred for them. They continually curse their fathers all their lives and eventually end up in prison simply because they couldn't handle their hurts. I seldom talk to an inmate who doesn't tell me how he hates his father. Because of this hatred, they have become violent and aggressive—cursing-mad at the world.

Reversing Your Hurts

Too many people seem to want to nurse, rehearse, or curse their hurts! Every time you see them, all they want to do is tell you how terrible everything is with them. The Christian idea is to reverse the hurt. The blacks have done this in their slogan, "Black is Beautiful." Rather than saying, "I'm inferior," they're saying, "My so-called weakness is really my strength."

In 2 Corinthians 12:10 we read, "Therefore, I take pleasure in infirmities, in reproaches, in necessities, in persecutions, in distresses for Christ's sake: for when I am weak, then am I strong." Paul says not to nurse and rehearse a hurt, but to reverse it. We need to learn to make our hurts our strengths. In our physical weakness, we gain a spiritual strength. Paul had a thorn in the flesh, and God used it to make him spiritually strong.

Sooner or later, every one of us is going to have a hurt. If we take it as a Christian should, we will reverse that hurt and make it a strength. We have to say that everything which happens to us is at least in the permissive will of God. But I wouldn't go so far as the fellow who fell down three flights of stairs, got up, brushed himself off, and said, "I thank the Lord I got that over with!"

In reading biographies, I have noticed that the people who have accomplished great things have, almost without exception, been people who have gone through terrible hurts. They have merely reversed their hurts, making them strengths! Rather than saying, "I went downhill ever since I had that problem," they say, "I have allowed that problem to prod me toward my goal." Over the kitchen sink, my wife has placed a sign that says, "Thank the Lord anyhow!" What does she mean? She has discovered that in her weakness, there is God's perfect strength. She can allow her problems to make her strong.

Rafer Johnson was born with a club foot but became one of the greatest decathlon champions of all time. I have yet to read a biography of a successful man or woman with a hurt whose push to overcome that hurt was not a factor in their success.

We can almost make a hard and fast rule that when someone fights to overcome a hurt, they gain the momentum that carries them far beyond those who exert only a minimal effort. By fighting to overcome a handicap, they build a momentum which takes them much higher than those who give only the normal effort. The seeds of your victories are hidden in your adversities.

The Ultimate Motivators

Merely *wanting* something is not enough to cause us to make the necessary sacrifices to attain it. The super effort is exerted when there is not only the *pull* of desire, but the *push* of discontent. Hurts can become our "pushers" that drive us toward our goals. They fuel our rockets and propel us through the clouds and to our goals. We travel light-years faster when we have the emotional build-up of discontent. To make a successful trip, we must also have a focus—a goal. Otherwise we may sit on the launchpad for the rest of our lives and simply fizzle, stewing in our own juices. But by directing the hurt toward our clear-cut goals, we'll soon be in orbit, speeding toward our objectives. Our guidance system is totally reliable, guiding us swiftly toward the thought which is currently dominant in our minds. The pull of desire and the push of discontent will give us double assurance of attaining our dreams. Our strengths are reinforced by our weaknesses, so that our disadvantage becomes our advantage.

How to Make Discontent an Ally

Discontent will help develop an "I'll show 'em" attitude. Often minority races have proved this in sports. Boxers and football and basketball players have, in these tough contact sports, shown an "I'll show 'em" drive.

There is also this attitude among Christian athletes. Even though I am a Christian, I can play a rough brand of football. In fact, as a Christian, I ought to play an even rougher brand than anyone else. I represent the greatest cause on earth, and I should represent this cause with excellence in sports. Obviously, I would play fair and square, but tough.

It has been said that if you take all of the minority races and all the Christians (some of whom are minority races, of course) out of pro football, you don't have much left. This is also true of other sports. These players have the push and pull that assures intensity!

This positive tension can be utilized as a source of long-term strength. Or, it can be activated in a pressure-packed moment to catapult us toward our goals.

By visualizing our goals and verbalizing the source of discontent, we get a power surge that can just make the difference between a fine person and a great one. As I said before, spectacular success is always preceded by unspectacular preparation. The everyday drudgery of getting in shape is an important part of the formula of success. It's this extra effort that gets us ready for the crisis performance when the pressure is on.

Praying for a Hurt?

Should we pray to get hurt so we can use that to become our strength? No, I don't think so. The hurts will inevitably come. They can't be avoided. We need to be concentrating on how we will correctly handle that hurt when it does come! Life is a grindstone. It will either gall and irritate us, or it will polish us and make us better for having gone through it.

The Great Squash Experiment

A university study was recently done on a plain, ordinary garden squash. A metal band with a pressure gauge was attached to the squash. Amazingly, the pressure soon went over 500 pounds, and kept increasing until it reached 2,000 pounds. Afraid that the metal band would break, the students replaced it with a stronger one. The pressure gradually rose to 5,000 pounds, and the squash burst. When the students cut open the squash, they discovered an extraordinary situation. The interior of the squash was fibrous and almost muscular in texture. When they dug into the soil and uprooted the plant, they found about 80,000 feet of cumulative root system that this plain little squash had formed! Although it had originally been a common garden squash, it had developed an altogether different type of interior and root system against adversity. It had reached down further and pushed out harder and developed an inner strength that was unheard of in any other squash. Why? Because it was fighting this external imprisonment.

I have discovered that the really great men and women are those who have a terrible obstacle to surmount. When they fight to overcome the pain, they reach down further and pull up harder and accomplish more than normal, all because of the problem.

It is inevitable that you will have a hurt. It will either make you bitter or better. You can either nurse, rehearse, and curse it, or you can reverse it to make it become your strength. It's up to you.

A Con Learned to Reverse His Hurt

In Eddyville, Kentucky, at the Kentucky State Penitentiary, I met a man in Maximum Security. He was a big West Kentucky hillbilly who was known as the toughest man in the joint. He'd killed three men with his bare hands. Many of his friends encouraged me to go down and talk to him. I descended three flights of stairs, went through four locked doors, and finally stood outside his cell. Inside I found a man with a very soft heart which had been buried beneath a rather thin veneer of hardness. He'd been in that six-by-eight-foot cell for four years when I first talked to him. That day he committed his life to Jesus Christ. And later he assured me that the greatest thing that ever happened to him was being locked in that six-by-eight-foot cell because only in that cell had he been able to stop long enough to see his need for the Lord. The last I heard, he was growing as a radiant Christian and had learned to reverse the hurt of being imprisoned by making even that six-by-eight-foot cell a strength.

I Learned to Reverse Hurt

My wife's little sign over the sink is an assurance that everything *bad* in our lives has always turned out to be *good*. I agree wholeheartedly!

I remember being traded from the Detroit Lions to the Cleveland Browns. I loved Detroit and did not relish the idea of going to play for Cleveland. I thought it was a terrible day when I was traded. However, it turned out to be the best thing that ever happened to me! I had my best years of football with the Browns.

Joseph Reversed Hurt

Joseph says it all when talking to his brothers who had sold him into slavery. He said, "Ye thought evil against me; but God meant it unto good" (Gen. 50:20). The important thing is not the intention of those who inflict the evil, nor the circumstances that surround the evil thing befalling us, but the way in which we handle it. God can allow everything that happens to us to gravitate toward our good if our attitude is like Joseph's, and we "thank the Lord anyhow!"

Bobby's Greatest Strength

My son, Bobby, was a fine football player in high school. Although he had a great junior year, halfway through his senior year he developed a massive hip infection. He was in horrible pain. All the blood tests indicated that an infection was present, but the doctors were unable to successfully stop it. Exploratory surgery was performed, and his appendix was removed. Still, there was no precise way to find the location of the infection.

It could be controlled with antibiotics, but the infection always returned when the medicine was discontinued.

Although there was great pain in Bobby's hip, the emotional pain of not being able to play football was much worse. Try as they would, the doctors were baffled! Finally, after a year and a half, they discovered in his sacroiliac (hip) joint a hole the size of a quarter. The infection had eaten this hole, and now it appeared that Bobby would never be able to play football again.

As I mentioned in a previous chapter, Bobby had accepted a football scholarship to Baylor University. His frustration was intense, as he thought of giving up his life-long dream.

Since the infection began to work on him early in his senior year of high school, he played in only the first three games. Grant Teaff, the head coach at Baylor University, gave him a scholarship based on his great showing as a high school junior. Even late in his senior year, the hip still gave him great pain. Teaff said, "We just believe he'll recover with God's help and become a great one."

He had built his upper body to incredible strength by constant weight lifting, but his legs were undeveloped because he had to rest the hip. The best medical opinion was that he would have to rest his hip and allow the hole to fill in by itself.

Obviously, he received some needling from Baylor teammates and even nonplaying students about getting a "free ride" because he was on full scholarship and not playing. This built a tremendous discontent. He became increasingly determined to "show 'em." But at the same time, he was growing even closer to the Lord. He prayed daily for physical healing and committed the results to the Lord. This waiting, working (weight lifting on his upper body only, and no running), and praying continued for two long years.

Bobby and I went to Baylor just before the football season of the second year. We told Coach Teaff that Bobby could no longer accept a football scholarship. The doctors had said that the only hope for full healing was to rest for another year. This would give his hip a chance to heal by itself. Grant was in complete agreement that Bobby should rest for the year. But he hesitated and his silence gained our full attention. When he did speak it was to say, "I have one major disagreement. Bobby will not go off scholarship as long as he is at Baylor. I'll expect him to be out for spring training, and I believe that God is going to allow him to get well and play for us."

The "I'll show 'em" attitude was now mixed with love for a coach that had stuck with him during his darkest hours. A closeness to Christ, growing out of his hurt, had filled him with faith that God would give him victory. We had traveled to Baylor with heavy hearts and crumbled dreams. But we were returning jubilantly, in absolute faith, with the gloom lifted from our hearts.

The following spring the hip was healed, and Coach Teaff's faith in God and in Bobby was vindicated. Bobby played sensationally, and he is now on his way to football greatness. (Perhaps this is a prejudiced father's opinion!) But at least, we certainly know that Bobby has reversed his hurt to make it a strength.

Within three weeks of that first year back in football, he moved from third- to first-string tackle and was a big part of a great Baylor championship season.

What good thing can God bring out of this supposed hurt that you are facing? This is the question you should ask yourself when facing adversity. Christ's greatest hurt became his and mankind's greatest victory. The wicked world crucified him, but Jesus, like Joseph, reversed what they "meant for evil" to the salvation of the world!

How to Make This Step on the Ladder Work

1. Hurts will come in your life, so learn to handle them.
2. Don't nurse and rehearse your problems, or even curse them.
3. Reverse your hurts and make them your strengths. In 2

Corinthians 12:10 we read that the Christian is to be thankful for his problems because they ultimately become his strengths.

4. Remember that motivation is the pull of desire and the push of discontent.

7.

GO THE SECOND MILE

The Seventh Rung on the Ladder Is to Go the Second Mile

Ultimately, dreams must have the hard stuff of reality in them. Otherwise, they simply float like clouds. They are fluffy and light, but only puff with no substance from which a life can be built.

As I mentioned in an earlier chapter, the great statesman and financier, Bernard Baruch, when asked the secret to his great success said, "I decided what I really wanted to be, and then I had to decide what I was willing to pay to achieve it."

It doesn't help to say we want to achieve great things unless we are willing to work hard and sweat to accomplish them. Athletic greatness demands sweat to reach that goal. Spiritual growth comes only if one is willing to humble himself and serve God with his whole heart and life. As we discussed earlier, spectacular success is always preceded by unspectacular preparation. There isn't any easy way.

None of us likes hard work. We are naturally lazy. Some of us like to loaf. Others like to overeat, but that won't get the job done. Sooner or later, we must discipline ourselves to get into action. That means doing some things we don't want to do. Alexander Hamilton said, "What people have ascribed to me as being genius is really only the product of hard work."

Make Hard Work a Game

As a little boy growing up in Alabama, Jim Brown began to imagine what it would be like to be the greatest fullback that ever lived: How would he talk? How would he eat? How much rest would he get? How much exercise would he take? How would he react in this situation and that? As a five-year-old boy, he already had become the greatest fullback that ever lived because he saw himself as that very person. And he started then to add action to his imagination. He started to do all the things the greatest fullback who ever lived would do. Every action of life was taken with one thing in mind—"what would the greatest fullback who ever lived do?" Soon the natural thing to him was to move like a guided missile toward his ideal. There was hard work, but it was all part of his childhood fantasy.

One day he awoke to find himself in New York Yankee Stadium. His fantasy had become a reality. With the look of a wide-eyed, five-year-old boy Jim explained to me how he had been guided by his dream. "It was so real to me. It was like a stage play. I saw it all before it ever happened." It had all begun when he was just a boy, as he started to do everything necessary to become the greatest fullback who ever lived.

Similar use of the imagination is now being used as a technique for treating alcoholics. "Role-playing" has been one of the most successful forms of recovery for alcoholics. In role-playing the alcoholic plays like he isn't an alcoholic, or like he has conquered it. He thinks of himself in situations like coming in after work and being met at the door by his loving wife and children. Or he pictures himself at a company party and he says "no" to the many offers of cocktails.

The same type of thing is done with the mentally ill. An individual with a mental problem imagines that he has no problem. Every effort is made to get realism into the role-playing situation. The patient then carries this new self image over into reality. At first, he feels unnatural and even hypocritical. But if he persists in playing the person he wants to be, he is soon that very person!

The Law that Makes Dreams Come True

When we begin to do the things the leaders in our fields of pursuit are doing, we are well on our way to making our goal a reality. But Christ always went one step further. He knew the secret of making dreams become the hard stuff of life. In the Sermon on the Mount, he said, "If someone forces you to go one mile, go with him two miles" (Matt. 5:41, NIV). What did he mean by that? There was an obnoxious Roman law that said any Roman government official or soldier could order any citizen of a conquered nation to carry his luggage one mile, and the citizen was bound to obey. It was law.

For instance, here comes a Roman soldier by a Jewish farm. The farmer is out working in the field. The Jews have recently been conquered by the Romans, so the soldier says to the farmer, "Hey, boy! Come here and carry my luggage!" The farmer goes over, picks up the luggage, and carries it one mile. Now there are one-mile markers all over that part of the world, because every farmer had a marker exactly one mile from his farm. He didn't want to carry that luggage one inch farther than he had to. So, this farmer would carry it one mile to the marker and drop it. He'd mumble through clenched teeth, "One of these days, we're gonna beat you Romans. When we do, I'm gonna make you carry my luggage ten miles!" The farmer would stomp back to his field, pick up his hoe, and resume his chopping with such fierceness that he'd break the hoe. He'd start home that night, and his wife would see him in the distance and know that he was gonna be hard to live with. Sure enough, he'd kick the dog, spank the kids, fuss at the wife, and bite everyone's head off.

But now the Master comes along and teaches the Law of the Second Mile. So, here comes this Roman soldier and he says, "Hey, you! Come here and carry my luggage one mile!" The farmer runs and jumps the fence, grabs the luggage, and carries it one mile—picks up speed and carries it two. He's almost into town when the Roman soldier finally says, "Why did you carry my luggage two miles? You carried it more than twice what you're supposed to. What's wrong with you?" "Oh," he says, "I don't mind. I may never get to Rome, and I'm enjoying just talking to you about it. I don't mind at all." As they part, the Roman soldier yells, "Hey, if you ever get to Rome, look me up. You're all right!"

And it works today. Here's a man putting on his coat in the morning, and he sees that a button is off. He says to his wife, who's washing dishes, "Dear, would you mind sewing this button on my coat?" She says, "Sew that button on your coat? You knew that button was off last night. Why didn't you tell me to do it then? You waited five minutes till you've gotta leave, and you ask me to sew a button on your coat. Give it to me!" She sews it on, mad enough to explode. She gets through, throws the coat at him, and says, "Here! Next time, tell me the night before, so I don't have to stop washing dishes to sew on your button. I have a schedule, too, you know. But you don't care anything about my schedule or what I have to do!" And she's still fussing as he sneaks out the door like a whipped puppy.

Later he comes home. She says, "Honey, I'm twenty dollars overdrawn. Could you loan me twenty?"

"Twenty dollars? I can't believe it! Your bankbook is always overdrawn. You're the worst manager in town. Here! Here's the twenty, but don't ever do that again!" he says. He's gone the first mile, but not one inch further. He wanted to eat, so he gave her the money.

But let's introduce the Law of the Second Mile to the twentieth century. The guy comes in just before he has to leave and says, "Darling, the button's off my coat. Would you sew it on?"

"Sure! I'd love to help you. Give me the coat." Even though her morning schedule is hectic, she takes the time to sew on the button. When she's through, she helps him on with the coat and sends him off with a kiss. He's ten feet tall all day because he's got a wife that understands the Law of the Second Mile.

Later in the week, he comes home from work one afternoon and is greeted with the request, "Sweetheart, would you loan me twenty dollars? I'm overdrawn."

"Twenty dollars? I can't believe it. Everyone else is spending twice what they used to in these inflationary times. You're only spending twenty dollars more. Why, you must be the world's best manager. Here's forty. You might need an extra twenty." She feels like a queen because she has a husband who understands the Law of the Second Mile.

Think what this would do for labor/management relations! If every employer gave twice what was expected of him and every employee gave twice what was expected of him, we would see a different story. I see a lot of people who do as little as they can possibly get by with. Some men go to work every day, then work hard all day long to avoid it. As Christians, we should strive to keep the Law of the Second Mile whether we are employees or employers. That means giving an honest day's work for an honest day's wages and then a little extra.

Think what this would do in the athletic world. Those who do twice what is expected of them athletically become the great ones. And so will you in your field of pursuit if you do twice what's expected of you. Remember, one plus one doesn't equal two in this case, but a multiplication of results. When you put forth a second-mile effort, it comes back multiplied! Whether negative or positive, it will always proliferate and come back to you in just the way you sent it out.

Those men who work hard all day to avoid work have the objective of not seeing how much they can do, but how little they can get by with doing. This is so much the case in American industry and business that the dedicated, disciplined, second-mile effort is so unique that it is often rewarded. If the second-mile person can withstand the resistance of fellow-workers or the thoughtlessness of some employers, he will rise to the top like cream. And you can do the same. If you want to succeed, don't get tight and nervous, just double your effort.

I convinced my sons of this, and as I expected, they achieved outstanding success. They worked out with their teams two hours daily, then ran three miles home and lifted weights. Luke 6:38 says, "Give, and it shall be given unto you; good measure, pressed down, and shaken together, and running over, shall men give into your bosom. For with the same measure that ye mete withal, it shall be measured unto you again." This idea of giving and having it multiplied and given back to you is just as true in relation to work and service as it is in giving money.

Admitting Wrong and Seeking Forgiveness

Although going the second mile is tough, many times it's difficult even to go the first mile. It's not easy, for instance, to admit when we're wrong. But think what this simple practice could mean in our personal relationships. If every father, for example, would remember to say "I'm sorry; I made a mistake; please forgive me," children would probably be much different than they are. I've found it works miracles with my own children to admit when I am wrong. Say one of my children wrecks the car, and I lose my temper and yell at him. To say, "I want you to forgive me because I know I was wrong when I yelled at you" is a big step for me. Now, the child was wrong in wrecking the car, but I was wrong in losing my temper and yelling. It's tough to say. You have to blurt such a statement. "I want you to forgive me because I yelled at you for wrecking the car." Think what a man it takes to say to his wife, "I want you to forgive me because I lost my temper." Think what a woman it takes to admit to her husband that she's been wrong. Think what it will do when you start being big enough to admit when you're wrong!

The big word here is *blurt*. If you don't "blurt," it will stick in your throat. You'll never quite get it out otherwise. Rehearse what you're going to say in your mind, and just spit it out. Even if you stumble over the words, they want to hear it so badly it will sound better than the Gettysburg Address.

We waste too much emotional energy on unresolved human

conflicts just because we're not big enough to ask for forgiveness. Maybe we were only 10 percent wrong and the other person was 90 percent wrong, but we're only responsible for our share of the guilt.

Ask for forgiveness. No man ever stands quite so tall as when he bows and asks forgiveness of his children, wife, friends, enemy, or anyone else.

What we've been discussing to this point is actually First Mile Christianity. As tough as it may be to admit when we're wrong, we really haven't pushed on beyond the first mile. We only break that barrier when we give the keys to our new car to the child who banged up the other one. Thus, in spite of his mistake, we've shown our trust in him though he doesn't necessarily deserve our confidence.

There remains yet one more step in going the second mile—that's to develop an attitude of caring and forgiveness toward our enemies. Second Mile Christianity is difficult with loved ones, but miraculous with enemies. Only the Lord can give us the stuff to turn an enemy into a friend. Asking forgiveness from an enemy, when he was the one who was more wrong, and helping him after he's hurt us, these are the ingredients of the hard-work struggle of going the second mile.

Never forget at the end of the second mile there awaits a joy and reward (though not always immediately obvious) beyond all we can imagine!

How to Handle Pressure

The human body can take a tremendous amount of stress. I played twenty-two years of football, twelve as a pro and ten in school. I wasn't injured badly enough to miss a game until the last part of that twenty-second year when I had a couple of ribs broken and had to miss the last four games of that year. Only once did I push myself too hard in a game—I passed out from heat exhaustion. Most of the time I paced myself too much. But the amazing thing about the body is that the harder you push it, the stronger it becomes. The more you stretch the body, brain, or soul, the more it grows.

In high-pressured jobs, such as sports, nervousness can become counterproductive. The athlete can't afford to choke. It short-circuits his abilities. The victory is dependent upon a 2½-hour period which comes only once a week. But what does the athlete do with all the other time the rest of the week? First, he works himself to the point of exhaustion so that he sleeps well and is too tired to be nervous about the upcoming game. However, as great as physical exertion is, there is a point of diminishing returns when we overdo it. A person's body can become so weary it needs complete rest in order to recover and grow stronger. But, as I said earlier, more often than not, we are usually too easy on ourselves.

When your body does need rest, concentrate on working your mind. Visualize yourself in vivid detail doing your job in winning form. Do this repeatedly. Anytime the job crosses your mind, make very sure it is in the form of powerful pictures. The second-mile work effort can move from the physical to the psychological, and more importantly, on to the spiritual. Make everything you do an object of prayer. "The effective prayer of a righteous man can accomplish much" (James 5:16, NAS).

In all his wisdom Solomon said, "With all of thy getting, get wisdom." But then came One wiser than Solomon who said, in essence, "with all of thy getting, get going." Action and second-mile effort must be added to words, thoughts and visions so that dreams become hard reality.

Like a determined farmer, you need to give your crop a chance to come up, then water and cultivate it. It won't happen overnight, but it will follow as certainly as the night follows the day. Your harvest is inevitable!

How to Make This Step on the Ladder Work

1. Remember that spectacular success is always preceded by unspectacular preparation.

2. Remember that dreams float like clouds until they are given substance by hard work. By acting out your dreams, they soon become the real thing.

3. Follow Christ's suggestion of going the second mile. Always go a step further. Doubled effort is tiring, but it multiplies results.

4. Start today picking out areas where you can double your giving of time, work, money, and self. Then watch God and man multiply and return your effort.

8.

LIVE THE FAITH
PHENOMENON

The Eighth Rung on the Ladder Is the Faith Phenomenon

The "Faith Phenomenon" is something we can see in every aspect of life. In the Bible, God is the object of our faith. He can and does reverse every circumstance if he chooses. And it is often done in direct proportion to our faith. However, I also believe that he has so made his universe that faith in almost any form is honored by God to help a person succeed. Obviously, a lack of faith assures failure. Faith in Christ is the best, because *it* assures success here and hereafter. But, faith in self, faith in others, faith in the principles of success, and so on are still effective toward our success. It's almost as if the whole of creation is pulling for the victory of faith. So, even the most pagan of people can experience success in life to a limited degree by utilizing belief. The most Christian of people have often sabotaged their own efforts by unbelief in themselves (God's creation) or unbelief in God. It is the prejudice of the Creator toward the positive that I choose to call the Faith Phenomenon. Even a little of it (mustard-seed size) is enough to move a mountain, a hill, a giant, or to save a soul.

A little boy and his sister began playing hide-and-seek in a department store while eating ice cream cones. As they became involved in the game, the ice cream began to melt. The youngsters were riding the elevator when the little boy looked down to see his ice cream melting all over his hand. Standing only inches in front of him was a lady wearing a fur coat. With one quick movement, he got rid of the melting ice cream by rubbing it into the mink coat. His sister, who was watching, voiced her concern by saying, "You're getting fur all in your ice cream." Obviously, the woman whose mink coat was being ruined lost her cool. There were three different points of view. The boy simply wanted to get the melted ice cream off his hand, his sister was worried about ice cream being ruined by the fur, and the woman was concerned about her expensive mink coat.

Where Are You Coming From?

Our preconceived ideas have a great deal to do with our point of view. The National Association for the Advancement of Colored People looks at things differently than the Ku Klux Klan. Labor looks at things in one way, and management in another. The power companies see through different eyes than the environmentalists. Some time ago, when the Three Mile Island nuclear accident occurred, the environmentalists yelled, "This proves nuclear power plants are dangerous! They're a threat to human existence! We came within an inch of seeing thousands of people injured or killed due to a radiation leak!" The power company officials said, "This proves once and for all that nuclear power is safe. Even in this worst of accidents no one was hurt." It was the same news event, but totally different responses.

As examples of different viewpoints in sports, take Pete Gent and myself. Pete Gent played with the Dallas Cowboys from 1964–1968. In his book *North Dallas Forty*, he sees the game through the eyes of a second-stringer who spent a lot of his time hurt. Consequently his viewpoint is mostly negative. His distorted view resulted in his magnifying only the bad aspects of the game. Once he caricatured Staubach as reading a Bible in the clubhouse prior to a game, a typical example of Gent's attempt to make Christianity appear to be stupid and not a live option for anyone but weirdos. In his thinking, most players off the field seem to be involved in a continuous orgy of sex, drugs, and alcohol. On the field, he lists all the standard abuses—some true and some not, but all overdone.

On the other hand, I played pro football from 1957 through 1968 and was always a starter. After playing with Detroit for four years, I went to Cleveland to play with the Browns until I retired in 1968. During those years I saw a lot of genuine Christians in pro football and less alcohol, drugs, sex, and other forms of corruption than in society as a whole. I was hurt only once, and I saw no one forced to play hurt.

So I viewed pro football as an exhilarating, challenging experience and a great opportunity to help people by using the platform it afforded to share my faith.

You Get Back What You Put Out

I recently heard of a service station owner who was approached by a motorist in his station, saying, "I'm looking for a new town in which to live. Could you tell me something about your town?" The service station owner said, "Sure. But first tell me a little about the town you came from."

"The town I left was filled with the most snobbish, narrow-minded, small-thinking, clannish people you can imagine. They were terribly unfriendly, and they made it difficult for a new person to feel wanted." The service station owner said, "You know, I've noticed that this town is very narrow-minded. They don't really let new people into their society very easily. They're often cold and unfriendly. In fact, I don't think you'd like this town."

The next day another motorist asked the same station owner the very same question. Again his reply was, "Tell me about the town you came from."

"Oh," the motorist said, "it was a great town. The people were very friendly. They accepted strangers in a very warm way.

It was a wonderful town." The station owner said, "Oh, well, I'm certain you'd like this town. It's a very friendly place. The people are warm, and they take strangers into their society quite easily and make them feel right at home." Having heard both conversations, one of the service station employees questioned the owner, "I don't understand. Just yesterday, you were telling a man that this town was very narrow-minded, unfriendly, and cold, and that these people didn't accept strangers. Now you tell this man the exact opposite!" The owner said, "Oh, don't you understand? A town reflects the attitudes we bring to it."

I know a lot of people who look at their jobs with the attitude: "I'm going to see how little I can get by with doing and still get paid." They look at their jobs in a narrow sort of way, and as a result, they never see their jobs as opportunities to accomplish great things.

I once read about a man who asked several bricklayers what they were doing. The first replied, "I am trying to make enough money to feed my hungry kids." The second said, "I'm laying these lousy bricks! Can't you see?" The third replied, "I'm building a great cathedral." The man who was building the cathedral will obviously be most motivated and effective in his job.

There is also the story of the man who worked hard all day long pouring concrete. Finally he smoothed the concrete to what he felt was perfection. Exhausted, he went into his house to sit down and relax. While drinking a glass of iced tea, he happened to look out the window to see ten or fifteen children gathered around the edges of the newly poured slab. No doubt, they were writing their names in the wet concrete. He stormed out of the house, yelling and screaming, scattering the children in all directions. Sometime later after smoothing out the concrete once again, he returned to the house, to his tea and his easy chair. Seeing his aggravation, his wife said, "Just yesterday, you told me that you loved children. Today, you're screaming and yelling and cussing at them." The man replied, "Oh, I do love children in the abstract, but not in the concrete." It's easy to love people in the abstract, but difficult to love them in the concrete situations of life. It's all a matter of viewpoint.

The Viewpoint of Christ

If only we could see the world through Jesus' eyes. I often wonder what he saw when he looked upon his surroundings. Did he see things as we would see them? In Mark 13:1, we'd be led to think that he saw things totally differently. His disciples said, "Look at this huge temple! What a fantastic structure it is—the most massive and the most beautiful in the world." Christ said, "Seest thou these great buildings? There shall not be left one stone upon another, that shall not be thrown down." In other words, he was saying that the temple was simply physical and wasn't nearly so important as spiritual things. He saw things through different eyes.

In my prison work, I try to tell the inmates that they should try to look at prison life through different eyes—to see it as an opportunity to better themselves. Many of them do. They lift weights, strengthen themselves, run, get their bodies in shape. Many study and some even earn graduate degrees. They strengthen their minds. Others study God's Word and grow spiritually. They even help each other grow in the Lord. Still others simply try to get themselves into the prison power structure and avoid being murdered, but they have little concern about making their time in prison productive.

"Stone walls do not a prison make, nor iron bars a cage." In other words imprisonment can be a state of mind. There are those who are walking free on the streets, but they are imprisoned in their minds.

There are those who are incarcerated in maximum security prisons, but are free within themselves! We can choose what our inner vision will be. We can choose whether we will give ourselves to thoughts of victory or thoughts of defeat and misery.

Jack Dempsey was going to fight Gene Tunney for the World Championship a number of years ago. The papers continued to say that Dempsey was literally going to knock Tunney's head off. Gene Tunney read all these reports. He seldom picked up a newspaper without finding an account of his impending destruction. One night very late, he awoke in terror, screaming at the top of his voice. In his nightmare he'd been decapitated. Dempsey had hit him so hard he'd knocked his head right out into the second row of seats. Tunney was trembling and in a cold sweat. He knew he must do something, so he quit reading the paper and began visualizing himself beating Dempsey. Several weeks later, to the amazement of the whole world, he did just that!

David's Faith

We can choose to have either a faith viewpoint or one of unbelief. There is a phenomenon in faith, one that has a great deal to do with the way we view the world. David looked at things differently than did Goliath. The big giant depended on his own strength. For him fighting was to be done with swords and spears, helmets, shields, leggings, breastplates—all of brass. But David's trust was in God. . . . God would enable him to use his abilities—his youth and speed, his skill with the slingshot—to perfection.

David was different. He had an attitude of faith! He knew that circumstances don't defeat, but that defeat or victory came as a result of our inner perception of those circumstances. Our viewpoint makes all the difference.

Goliath thought, "I am a giant. I am covered completely. David's just a boy, and there's no way he's going to beat me!" So he laughed in overconfidence at this upstart of a kid without any armor. "I'm powerful Goliath!" he bellowed.

What Goliath didn't realize was that David was young and fast. Rather than seeing the giant all covered with armor, David thought to himself, "His forehead is wide open. He's slow and I'm young and fast. If I couldn't hit that big forehead, I might as well give up! I've been killing wild animals on the run. How could I miss that big, wide, open forehead? After all, the Lord is with me." The army of Israel and King Saul thought David didn't have a chance, but he was the only one who had the courage to fight the giant. The Philistine army was gagging in laughter at this little runt of a kid attempting to fight big Goliath. So, everyone had a different viewpoint. David ran swiftly into battle with only his slingshot flying in the air. He shouted in the phenomenal faith of the Lord, "I come to you in the power of God and you come to me with sword and shield! God will be victorious!" And that he was! As the slingshot zinged the rock that hit dead center between the eyes of the great giant, Goliath fell to the ground and David was the victor!

This is a phenomenal sort of faith and the kind that God can honor. Winners expect to win; they believe in advance. They have the eyes of faith. "Believing, yet having not seen . . . ," that's what faith is all about. Moses had this faith. By faith, he had to get his feet wet in the Red Sea before God parted the waters and allowed the people of Israel to cross on dry ground. He had to act on his faith before anything would happen.

This is what it means to "practice your faith." You visualize in advance what God is going to do and how you are going to be used to accomplish this great thing. This kind of faith conditions your mind, and conditions the will of God. God honors such faith. In Hebrews 11, the words *by faith* appear over and over again. "By faith," great things were accomplished in the lives of the saints of God. They had a peculiar kind of faith which God honored in victories.

There is a unique power that flows toward those who believe God can do anything through them. When we get in line with this tremendous flow of God, great things can happen. Even unbelievers work on somewhat the same principle. That is, they visualize a positive outcome. Mohammed Ali and Jim Brown, for example, aren't Christians. Nevertheless, they use the principle of positive thinking. That is to believe the best in advance and it will happen. A lot of non-Christians are using these principles to accomplish non-Christian goals. What we need is Christian people using Christian principles to accomplish Christian goals! This can be done when we begin to believe that God can and will work through us. Of course, the ultimate is for Christians to use these principles for good.

Reliable Failure

Believing the outcome before it happens in everything we do can backfire. When we think in negative images, the outcome will be negative. In prisons, I've noticed inmates who have tattooed on their bodies, "Born to Lose." In fact, I've seen this on hundreds of inmates, and I think that's not only tattooed on their bodies but also on their brains. If we think we're born to lose, we will.

I spoke with one inmate who had tattoos all over his body. The most horrible of all was one emblazoned on his chest and stomach. It covered the entire front of his body. It was a vulgar middle-finger sign. I asked, "Why?" He said, "Because that's my attitude toward the world." As we talked further, I discovered that the world had taken that same attitude toward him. He got back something of the same "vibes" he was putting out.

Self-Fulfilling Prophecy

The outcome of negative programming is just as predictable as that of positive programming. We can program ourselves to fulfill our worst fears. My wife and I were recently counseling with a woman whose marriage was breaking up. She said after hours of desperate, pessimistic talk, "My grandmother's husband deserted her. At first, her marriage seemed great, but after about ten years he took off, leaving her alone and bitter. Believe it or not, the exact same thing happened to my mother when my father deserted her after ten years. Now the thing I've always feared has happened to me! Ten years of marriage have ended in the same way for me as they did for my mother and grandmother. The thing I dreaded most happened to me." Faith worked in reverse for her. It was a recurring unbelief coming to life.

Christian people are called "simplistic, naïve, unrealistic," and the world thinks they ignore reality. I have talked with many people who are very intimate with Billy Graham, and I've known him myself for some time. The only criticism I've ever heard of him is that he's "simplistic, naïve, and unrealistic, and he ignores reality." The fact of the matter is that he has Christian faith, and this world is cynical and unbelieving; therefore, the world doesn't understand a man of this kind of faith. Even in the time of Jesus, faith of this kind was misunderstood. In Matthew 9:18, 23–25 we read of a certain ruler whose daughter died. He went to Jesus and asked him to perform a miracle of resurrection. Because of this man's faith, Jesus went to his house and said to the mourners, "The little girl is just asleep." But they laughed him to scorn. The ruler believed that Christ could make her live. But the unbelieving mourners saw her dead. Because of her father's phenomenal faith in Christ, the girl lived.

How do you see the world? In belief or unbelief? The scribes and Pharisees looked at their world in unbelief. Jesus was not as the scribes and Pharisees, but looked at the world with the belief of One having authority.

Many times while working in prisons, I have seen that the chaplains and administrators look at the inmates in unbelief. They think nothing good can happen to the inmates. They think change is not possible in the lives of these men. They think human nature is such that it cannot be changed. In our ministry, an attitude of faith is one of the things we bring to these institutions. We believe that God can change people because he can change human nature. Christ saw individuals for what they could become.

Hebrews 11 records the faith of the saints. In studying the life of each saint we discover they have a lot of skeletons in their closets. If you catalogued their crimes, you would find there is hardly a crime committed by a man in prison today that wasn't committed first by the saints of God. Samson did most of them himself. Moses was a murderer. But by faith, they were transformed and changed. God takes criminals and uses them to accomplish fantastic things. He doesn't allow them to remain criminals. He changes them by rebirth and then uses them in great ways. Love has a way of seeing people at their best, in all their potentiality and with all their possibilities.

You know how they train elephants in Africa? They take the elephant and chain him to a tree—usually a banyan tree. These trees are huge with deep roots and great trunks. The strongest winds don't make the banyan tree quiver. The elephant will pull and jerk until his leg becomes very sore and bloody, but he won't wiggle the banyan tree or budge the steel chain at all. He simply hurts himself. He'll continue to pull and tug as long as three weeks against the chain. But finally he'll become still and give up. He knows he can't make the chain give and that the banyan tree will never bend. The elephant will never try again as long as he lives to pull against a chain. You can tie the other end of the elephant's chain to the smallest tent stake. He could pull that little stake out by the simple flex of one muscle, but he'll never try. He's certain that in reality there is a banyan tree at the other end of the chain, rather than a tent stake.

There is a faith phenomenon that says, "We expect to win in advance, and we will. We believe, yet having not seen. We have the eyes of faith. We know that the very best is going to happen because we, like David, are going into battle with the power of God." This faith phenomenon enables us to look at our world altogether differently than others do and to believe that all things are possible.

When we adapt the faith viewpoint and see things as Christ did, victory will be ours.

John Oxenham in *The Vision Splendid* says,

> Blessed are they that have eyes to see,
> They shall find God everywhere.
> They shall see Him where others see stones.

How to Make This Step on the Ladder Work

1. Change the way you look at things. You can alter the situation! Remember, reality is altered by your viewpoint. Christ always looked at his world through eyes of faith. Why don't you try it?

2. See your world as it *can* be, and even the most difficult problem becomes an opportunity.

3. Choose what thought you want to give yourself to. The greatest freedom on earth is the freedom to choose your own attitude.

4. Expect to win in advance. This is the common denominator of all winners. Try cultivating that habit!

9.

NEVER GIVE UP

The Top Rung on the Ladder Is Never Give Up

The final rung at the top of the ladder to success is the capacity to overcome discouragement. There are times when we all want to throw in the towel—times when we want to stop pursuing our goals because "the going gets tough," but if we're going to realize our dreams we have to overcome the discouragement of setbacks no matter how many times they occur. Sometimes these problems may even lead us to set new goals because the old ones are no longer realistic. But whatever the case, we must develop an attitude that doesn't give up before we even get started—one that doesn't give in to discouragement.

Psychosclerosis

Arteriosclerosis is a hardening of the arteries. It is ultimately deadly, but not nearly so deadly as the terrible disease of "psychosclerosis," which is a hardening of the attitude. In France they say *"Ennui."* In England they say, "I really couldn't care less." In the United States we say, "So what?" But, wherever you see it all over the world, it is the same attitude of ingratitude.

The late Jean Paul Sartre, a French agnostic-existentialist who has probably had more influence on free-world thinking than any other single philosopher, entitled his autobiography *Nausea*. He came to a climactic point in the book where he said, "I have discovered that I am alive and it nauseates me." Wouldn't that be a terrible thing—to write your autobiography and call it *Nausea?* It's like writing your own life story and calling it *Vomit.*

Whatever else you may say of Christianity, it is a happy experience. It is a sin to be joyless. Christ came into the world so that we might have life, and have it more abundantly. Too often we have an attitude of ingratitude. The grass is always greener on the other side of the fence. "Somebody always has a better deal than I do. My situation is terrible! Poor me! I really have it bad!"

I heard about a guy who was constantly in trouble. Everything that happened turned out bad for him. His friends said, "You know what he needs? He needs a success experience. He has never been successful at anything. Let's rig a winning experience for him. We can put a bunch of numbers in a hat, and every number in the hat will be 'four.' Let's assign him the number 'four.' Then, when he picks the number out of the hat, it will have to be 'four.' " Everyone agreed that this was the thing to do. He was sure to win. Finally, he would have at least one success. The poor guy reached into the hat, pulled out a number and it was "6⅞." A lot of people can't win for losing.

You've heard about that minister who was arriving by airplane. He was a visiting minister, and no one knew what he looked like. The man sent to pick him up at the airport had never even seen a picture of him. As the passengers streamed off the plane the man watched carefully to see if he could pick out the visitor. After studying the face of each person who got off, he finally went up to a man and said, "Are you a minister?" The guy said, "No, I've been sick lately. That's why I look that way." Isn't it too bad that many people look at ministers in just that way? Christian leaders to them are sick-looking. The reverse should be true! They ought to be the picture of health and happiness. They are leaders of the most joyous faith on earth—that of Jesus Christ. Every lay person should be a happy person, as well. You see, Jesus didn't invite us to a funeral. He invited us to a wedding feast! "I am come that you might have life and that you might have it more abundantly" (John 10:10). His Gospel is good news! Good news! Something wonderful has happened. You have eternal life through Christ!

But life isn't always fun and games. It is often tragic and sad. Christ does make a happy commentary on life. What's more, he guides us to rise out of the ashes of sorrow to smell the roses again.

But sooner or later, discouragement will come to each of us or we will come to it. It is absolutely impossible to avoid. How do we overcome it? How do we attain Christian joy? I would say first of all, we need to remember who we are. We're creatures made in the image of God. We have fantastic worth within ourselves! We're in his image.

In the Image of God

"God created man in his own image, in the image of God created he him; male and female created he them" (Gen. 1:27). We were created in the image of God. Because of sin, that image was marred. But, by rebirth it is restored. In Colossians 3:9–10 we read, "ye have put off the old man with his deeds; and have put on the new man, which is renewed in knowledge after the image of him that created him." That demands a high standard of conduct and quality of life. A creature in the image of God by birth and rebirth must not violate his high calling.

You've probably heard about the baby tiger who got lost in a herd of goats. The tiger thought he was a goat. He nibbled green grass like the rest of the goats. He nursed the mother goat. He even made bleating noises like a goat rather than roaring like a tiger.

One day a big tiger came roaring through the herd of goats, and all the goats scattered in every direction, but for some unknown reason, the tiny tiger didn't run away. He just stayed there and was confronted by this huge, powerful tiger. The big tiger roared so loudly the ground quivered. The tiny little tiger bleated like a goat in reply. The big tiger could hardly believe his ears! He roared again, and all he got was another bleat. To his dismay, he saw that baby tiger nibbling green grass. He thought to himself, "This is horrible!" He jerked the baby tiger up by the nape of his neck took him down to a clear pool and suspended him over the water so he could see his reflection. When the baby tiger looked down, to his amazement, what he saw looked more like a tiger than a goat. He could hardly believe it. When the big tiger put him down, baby tiger once again began to bleat. But every time he made a bleating noise the big tiger cuffed him up-side the head. Before long he started making noises more like a tiger than a goat. Likewise, the baby tiger wasn't allowed to eat grass, but he was soon introduced to the taste of warm meat. It wasn't long until he began to act like a tiger. Why? Because when he was confronted with that which he was created to be, it brought out of him what he was intended to be.

When we are confronted with the Living God in Jesus Christ, it brings out of us that which we were meant to be. When we come into vital relationship with him, we begin to reflect him. I see a lot of people who have forgotten the image in which they were created. They drink until they're silly; they jump into bed with everybody they see; they puncture their veins with all sorts of drugs. They're acting like goats when God intended them to act like tigers. Remember who you are! You're a creature made in the image of God.

Christians are the most power-filled people in the world. "How incredibly great his power is to help those who believe him. It is that same mighty power that raised Christ from the dead . . ." (Eph. 1:19–20, TBL). Too many of us are operating on pennies, when God intended that we should utilize millions from his bank of power. It is too bad that we don't remember the tremendous power we have as Christians.

I look around sometimes on Sunday mornings and I think to myself, "Wouldn't it be wonderful if we in our churches could draw crowds like professional sports?" When I was with the Cleveland Browns, we drew 80 thousand in average attendance. Over 290 million people see all pro sports every year. There aren't that many people in the United States! So a lot of people are going to more than one pro sporting event. Wouldn't it be a great thing if we could draw crowds like that in our churches? No, it would be terrible because we already draw over 4.4 billion in church attendance in the United States each year. The worst thing that could happen to our churches would be for them to *only* draw an attendance like pro sports events. We already outdo them in attendance. In fact, we kill 'em! And sports fans only spend about 2 billion dollars a year on sports. We in the U.S. in a combination of all Christian causes, give more than 14 billion dollars a year. So, you see, we're not just a struggling little movement. We're a powerful force. We haven't done what we should, but we're making an impact on our country and on the world. But remember, success will only come if we *never give up* trying to be what God intended us to be.

Remember—You Have Been Forgiven

Some of the sweetest words Jesus ever said were *Tel Telesti* or "It is finished." When Christ died on the cross and rose again, it was a finished work. We have been forgiven!

But we must learn to act like we are forgiven. Our forgiveness is unconditional. We don't have to crawl around in the dirt and beg God to forgive us. He has already forgiven us by his life, death and resurrection. All he wants us to do is accept that forgiveness which he has already provided for us and appropriate it to our lives. It's already there. We need only to come in simple, childlike faith, and ask for it. Obviously, forgiveness isn't automatic. We must ask for it! God isn't saying, "If you'll agree never to do it again, then I'll forgive you." He's saying,

"Even though I'm sure you will do it again, I still forgive you, unconditionally!" In 1 John 1:8–9 we read, "If we say that we have no sin, we deceive ourselves, and the truth is not in us. If we confess our sins, he is faithful and just to forgive us our sins, and to cleanse us from all unrighteousness."

God Expects a Great Deal Out of You

Back in 1929, Georgia Tech was playing against the University of California in the Rose Bowl. Georgia Tech had a defensive end by the name of Roy Reigals. Roy rushed in from the defensive right side, charging headlong for the quarterback when he got blindsided. The hit was so hard that he became disoriented. About that time, someone deflected a pass which flew up in the air and came down in Roy's arms. The surprised Reigals took off at top speed, running for the goal line. He was thrilled! It was the first time he'd touched the ball all year, and now he was going to score. But on the three yardline after running 63 yards he was tackled by one of his own teammates. It was only then that he discovered he'd been running in the wrong direction. For the rest of his life he was known as "Wrong Way Reigals."

At halftime, totally dejected, he sat in one corner of the dressing room unwilling to even talk to his teammates. No one thought he'd even come back out to play the second half. They thought he'd just give up. To everyone's surprise not only did he come back out the second half, but he had the greatest half of his career. When the game was over, Roy was asked, "How did you do it? We didn't even think you'd have the courage to play the second half. Yet, you played the greatest half of your career!" His reply was, "Oh, that's simple. My coach came over to me as I was sitting in a corner by myself with my head down between my legs. I wanted to quit. But he grabbed me by the shoulders and pulled me up, looked me in the eye, and said something I couldn't shake. He said, 'Roy, I believe in you. I expect a great game from you!' I realized that if my coach believed in me, I couldn't let him down. So, I went back out and played with everything that was in me!"

When we think our lives are a mess, God grabs us by the shoulders, pulls us up, looks us dead in the eye, and says, "I believe in you, and I expect a great deal out of you. I want you to do something in my kingdom. I don't want you to act like a goat—I want you to act like a tiger for my sake!"

The Most Dangerous Place in Football

When I was a young football player, I'd get knocked down and I'd think, "This is a good chance to rest!" I would stay there and rest awhile. But, it wasn't long until I decided that really wasn't intelligent, because everytime I did this, I'd get trampled. So, I decided the most dangerous place on the field was on the ground. The safest place is up on your feet moving top speed toward doing your job. Players who get knocked flat on their backs or terribly off-balance end up making 80 or 90 percent of the tackles because they don't give up.

Many people give up the first time something goes wrong. When asked, "Are you really serving the Lord?" they say, "No, you see, there are a lot of people down there in that church that I don't like," or "No, those people in that church aren't very friendly to me, and that pastor says things that I don't like to hear. I like to sing in the choir, but they're not too nice to me. I like to play the piano, but they don't let me do it." There are a thousand and one excuses for not living for Christ—all ways of giving up. But if we want to achieve a successful Christian life, we must never give up.

When Your Feet Are Cut from Beneath You

All of his life, Dale Edison had dreamed of being a great pro football kicking specialist. From the time he was old enough to walk, he was out in his backyard kicking a little football over a bench. He got to where he could do that pretty well, so he started kicking it over the fence, and finally, the house. For San Diego State University in California, he kicked twenty consecutive field goals without a miss. He was the No. 2 draft choice for the San Diego Chargers, the highest draft choice for any football kicking specialist at that time. This was the fulfillment of his dreams. This was what he'd lived for, and now it was his!—a pro football kicking contract! He was so pleased that he got together some of his friends on the Fourth of July to celebrate his pro football contract by having a big explosion in his backyard. They stuffed a bunch of sulphur explosives into a milk can. In a freak explosion, both of his feet and one of his hands were blown off. This was the end of Dale Edison's dream of being a great pro football kicking specialist. Now he had no feet and only one hand. A lesser man would have given up—but not Dale!

I later learned that some of my books and records were an encouragement, both psychologically and spiritually to Dale in his recovery from this accident. Then one day several years ago, just as I was leaving for a speaking engagement in Sacramento, California, a friend called to tell me he had just heard Dr. Kenneth Cooper, who wrote the book *Aerobics*. In speaking on the subject of physical fitness, Dr. Cooper said, "I just got back from the San Francisco Marathon, and I was very impressed with the men who finished first, second, and third place in the race. But I was even more impressed by the ones who finished last, next to last, and third from the last. The man who finished last had no feet. But he never stopped once. He finished that 26-mile race running on the stubs of his ankles, cushioned by foam rubber. The man who finished second to last bragged that he only fell twice, but that wasn't too bad for a man who was totally blind. The man who finished third to last was no man at all, but a little nine-year-old girl." Dr. Cooper also talked of standing next to a man who told him he ran six miles every morning before breakfast. That wasn't too impressive until he told him he was 103 years old! This fellow also claimed to hold the 100-yard dash record—for men over 100!

When I got to Sacramento, I shared the story about the man who finished last and had no feet, but ran on the stubs of his ankles for twenty-six miles. What I didn't know was that Dale Edison was in my audience. He'd driven several hours to come and hear me speak that night. When I'd finished, Dale, who was walking on his new artificial feet, was the first young man I met. As he shook hands with me, using his left hand because he had no right hand, tears were streaming down his cheeks. Inspired by the story of the marathon runner who had no feet and with determination in his voice, Dale blurted out, "I'll never, never, never give up!"

Here was a man who had a goal of being a great pro football kicking specialist, and now he had no feet and only one hand. Yet, he just sets bigger, better goals and goes for them with all his heart. He's a leader in his church, his family, his business, and his civic life. In every area of his community, he leads because he refused to let adversity get him down. He wouldn't give up.

Since all of us will sooner or later get discouraged, the question is: How do we overcome it?

How to Make This Step on the Ladder Work

1. You must recognize discouragement when it comes. Label it as being anti-Christian and get out of it quickly, keeping in mind that Christians should be joyful.

2. Remember that you are made in the image of God; therefore, you're created for splendid dream fulfillment, not to grovel in the mud.

3. Remember you are unconditionally forgiven. If you accept God's loving forgiveness, there is no need for guilt.

4. The Lord expects great things out of you, so begin to expect greater things from yourself.

5. When you are tempted to give up, think of Dale Edison, the field goal kicker, who had both of his feet and a hand blown off, but who set new goals and went for them!

6. It's not really enough just to hang on. You've got to go one step further and make your hurts your strengths. You've got to let your problems prod you toward your goals in life. Determination is an important step on the ladder to your dreams. Without it you may give up too soon and fall short of your goals.

EPILOGUE

Remember what the junior high coach said to little Jessie Owens, "Dreams have a way of floating high in the sky like clouds and never becoming reality, unless you have the courage to build a ladder to them."

The only way I know to build a ladder to a dream is one rung at a time. The first rung of the ladder must be *what you think* because what you think has a peculiar way of becoming true in your life. The second rung is *what you say* because what you say becomes reality. The third rung is *being specific* because a clear-cut definite goal is a powerful force. Decide what you want to be physically, mentally, and spiritually. Write your goals down, decide exactly what you want to accomplish, and then go for them.

The fourth rung of the ladder is *responsibility*. Remember that you are responsible for both the victories and failures that take place in your life. The fifth rung is your *choice of friends*. Be the kind of friend who helps others by sharing their problems and victories. Then you will attract the same kind of friends— those who get excited with you about your goals. The sixth rung is *learning to handle your hurts*. You can reverse your hurts by making them strengths. The seventh rung on this ladder is the hard work of *going the second mile*. Ultimately hard work must be added to all the other steps on your ladder—imagination, words, goals, responsibility, friends, and hurts—before your dreams can become the hard stuff of reality. The eighth rung is to *live the faith phenomenon.* You will find that your expectations will actualize themselves.

The top rung of the ladder to your dreams is to *never give up.* There are occasions when we all want to stop too soon—times when we want to give up—but the ones who learn to "hang in there" will have the victory.

Start building your ladder now. And expect to win. One day you'll wake up and discover that your dreams have all come true.